ISBN 0-8373-6456-6

56 CERTIFIED NURSE EXAMINATION SERIES

 **RUDMAN'S QUESTIONS AND ANSWERS ON THE...**

Certified Nurse Registration Examination For...

Certified Nurse's Aide

D1316924

Test Preparation Study Guide
Questions & Answers

NATIONAL LEARNING CORPORATION

PASSBOOK®
NOTICE

PASSBOOK® SERIES

THE *PASSBOOK® SERIES* has been created to prepare applicants and candidates for the ultimate academic battlefield — the examination room.

At some time in our lives, each and every one of us may be required to take an examination — for validation, matriculation, admission, qualification, registration, certification, or licensure.

Based on the assumption that every applicant or candidate has met the basic formal educational standards, has taken the required number of courses, and read the necessary texts, the *PASSBOOK® SERIES* furnishes the one special preparation which may assure passing with confidence, instead of failing with insecurity. Examination questions — together with answers — are furnished as the basic vehicle for study so that the mysteries of the examination and its compounding difficulties may be eliminated or diminished by a sure method.

This book is meant to help you pass your examination provided that you qualify and are serious in your objective.

The entire field is reviewed through the huge store of content information which is succinctly presented through a provocative and challenging approach — the question-and-answer method.

A climate of success is established by furnishing the correct answers at the end of each test.

You soon learn to recognize types of questions, forms of questions, and patterns of questioning. You may even begin to anticipate expected outcomes.

You perceive that many questions are repeated or adapted so that you can gain acute insights, which may enable you to score many sure points.

You learn how to confront new questions, or types of questions, and to attack them confidently and work out the correct answers.

You note objectives and emphases, and recognize pitfalls and dangers, so that you may make positive educational adjustments.

Moreover, you are kept fully informed in relation to new concepts, methods, practices, and directions in the field.

You discover that you are actually taking the examination all the time: you are preparing for the examination by "taking" an examination, not by reading extraneous and/or supererogatory textbooks.

In short, this PASSBOOK®, used directedly, should be an important factor in helping you to pass your test.

CERTIFIED NURSE EXAMINATION SERIES

NURSING EXAMINATION RESOURCES

A variety of tests and programs are available through a number of organizations that will aid and help prepare candidates for nursing certification:

AMERICAN NURSES CREDENTIALING CENTER (ANCC)

The American Nurses Credentialing Center (ANCC) is a subsidiary of the American Nurses' Association (ANA), and the largest nursing credentialing organization in the United States. The ANCC Commission on Certification offers approximately 40 examinations including advanced practice specialties for nurse practitioners and clinical nurse specialists.

Certification is a most important way for you to show that you are among the best in your field – an extra step for you and your career, a step *beyond* state licensing. It gives you recognition and status on a *national* basis.

ANCC certification exams are offered twice a year in May and October in paper-and-pencil format, and throughout the year as computer-based exams. All exams are multiple choice and cover knowledge, understanding and application of professional nursing practice and theory. The time allotted for both the paper-and-pencil and computer certification exams is 3 hours and 30 minutes.

Each exam is developed in cooperation with an individual Content Expert Panel (CEP) composed of experts representing specific areas of certification. These panels analyze the professional skills and abilities required and then define which content should be covered and how strongly emphasized. Test questions are written by certified nurses in their discipline and reviewed by the ANCC to ensure validity and quality.

Exams are scored on a scale, and will be reported as either "Pass" or "Fail." Those who fail the exam will receive diagnostic information for each ꞏ ꞏ of the test. There is a minimum 90-day waiting period from the date ⁿᶠ ꞏꞏ   ᵐ for those looking to retake it. For those who pass the exᵃᵐ   ₑntification card and pin will be sent. Certification is vᵃˡᶤᵈ

For furthₑᵣ ꞏ   ꞏʳ
certification,

You caꞏ   rtification
exams and regꞏ   aling.org
– or by phone (ꞏ   an also
be found on the ꞏ   e test
as well as the coꞏ

NATIONAL CERTIFICATION CORPORATION

NCC CERTIFICATION

NCC – the National Certification Corporation for the Obstetric, Gynecologic and Neonatal Nursing specialties – is an independent certification organization. NCC was established in 1975 as a non-profit corporation for the purpose of sponsoring a volunteer certification program.

BENEFITS OF CERTIFICATION

Certification serves as an added credential to attest to attainment of special knowledge beyond the basic nursing degree. Certification serves to maintain and promote quality nursing care by providing a mechanism to nurses to demonstrate their special knowledge in a specific nursing area.

Promotion of quality care through certification benefits not only the individual nurse and the profession of nursing, but the public as well. Certification documents to employers, professional colleagues and health team members that special knowledge has been achieved, provides for expanded career opportunities and advancement within the specialty of OGN nursing, and elevates the standards of the obstetric, gynecologic and neonatal nursing practice.

Certification granted by NCC is pursuant to a voluntary procedure intended solely to test for special knowledge.

NCC does not purport to license, to confer a right or privilege upon, nor otherwise to define qualifications of any person for nursing practice.

The significance of certification in any jurisdiction or institution is the responsibility of the candidate to determine. The candidate should contact the appropriate state board of nursing or institution.

EXAMINATION DEVELOPMENT

NCC selects educators and practitioners in both nursing and medicine who possess expertise in the specialty areas within the obstetric, gynecologic and neonatal nursing and related fields to serve on the test committees. Responsibilities of the test committees include coordination of overall development of certification examinations and development of materials to assist candidates to assess readiness to participate in the certification process.

EXAMINATION DESCRIPTION

Each of the examinations consists of 200 multiple-choice questions. Two forms of each examination are often given to provide the opportunity to perform statistical procedures which ensure added reliability to the total examination process. The examinations are offered only in English and are designed to test special knowledge.

The examinations are given once each in the morning and afternoon, Monday through Friday, at more than 100 test centers. Four hours are allotted for completion of the examination.

THE CERTIFICATION PROCESS

1. Applicants must complete and file a certification application and appropriate documentation and fees
2. An acknowledgment postcard is sent to each applicant when NCC receives the application
3. Eligibility to participate is determined
4. Applicant is notified of eligibility status and eligible candidate receives a Candidate Guide to NCC Certification (4 to 6 weeks from receipt of application)
5. Candidates will schedule their own appointment for an examination time and location, and must take the exam within a 90-day period from notification of eligibility
6. Test administration occurs
7. Examinations are scored and analyzed
8. Candidates receive score reports upon completion of computerized testing (not paper testing)
9. Candidates are notified of certification status, receive information about certification maintenance and are later issued formal certificates

REVIEW COURSES AND NCC

NCC does not sponsor or endorse any review courses or materials for the certification examinations, because to do so would be a conflict of interest.

NCC is not affiliated with and does not provide input or information for any review courses or materials that other organizations may offer.

NCC views certification as an evaluative process. Eligibility criteria have been established to identify a minimum level of preparation for the exams.

CANDIDATE GUIDE TO NCC CERTIFICATION

Each candidate determined eligible to participate in the NCC certification process will be sent a Guide to NCC Certification. These guides can also be found online at the NCC website (www.nccnet.org). The Candidate Guides contain:

- General policies and procedures about the certification process
- Competency Statements that serve as a role description for the specialty nurse
- Expanded examination content outline
- Bibliography of references
- Sample questions to familiarize candidates with examination format (*These questions are not representative of exam content or difficulty level)

The Candidate Guide is not provided as study material, but to assist candidates in evaluating their own nursing practice as they prepare for the certification examination through identification of potential areas of strength and weakness.

SCORING OF EXAMINATIONS

Passing scores are determined based on a criterion-referenced system. Criterion passing scores are established by the NCC Board of Directors in conjunction with the NCC Test Committees using standard psychometric procedures.

Each question is statistically analyzed and evaluated with psychometric consultation, and scores are computed based on this evaluation.

Candidates who take the computerized form of the certification exam will receive their score reports upon completion of the exam. Those who take the paper/pencil exam will not receive their score reports for several weeks after administration.

NOTIFICATION AND AWARDING OF CERTIFICATION

Each candidate is notified of the success or failure to achieve certification. Successful candidates receive a formal certificate and will be able to use the initial RNC (Registered Nurse Certified) to indicate certification status.

Certification is awarded for a period of three years. Initial certification is effective from the date of notification to December 31 of the third full calendar year following notification. Subsequent periods of certification are subject to policies of the Certification Maintenance Program.

CERTIFICATION MAINTENANCE

The NCC Certification Maintenance Program allows the certified nurse to maintain NCC certification status.

Certification status must be maintained on an ongoing basis every three years through demonstration of approved continuing education or reexamination. Certification that is not maintained through the Certification Maintenance Program may only be regained by reexamination.

Specific information about the Certification Maintenance Program is provided to successful certification candidates and may also be obtained by contacting the NCC website (www.nccnet.org).

GENERAL POLICIES

All required practice experience/employment must have occurred while the applicant is/was a U.S. or Canadian RN. Graduate Nurse or Interim Permit status is acceptable, but must be indicated separately on the application form in addition to original licensure information.

NCC defines employment as practice in any of the following settings: direct patient care, educational institutions, administration or research.

When meeting educational requirements, all coursework, including that not directly related to specialty areas, thesis work and/or other program requirements must be completed at the time the application is filed.

It is the policy of NCC that no individual shall be excluded from the opportunity to participate in the NCC certification program on the basis of race, national origin, religion, sex, age or handicap.

All applications received are subject to the nonrefundable application fee ($250 paper/pencil; $300 computer).

Incomplete applications or applications submitted without appropriate fees will be returned and subject to all policies, fees and deadlines.

Applicants determined eligible (whether the candidate has been notified or not) and withdrawn will be subject to stated refund policies.

All NCC policies and requirements are subject to change without notice.

RETEST POLICIES

The NCC does not limit the number of times a candidate may retake the NCC Certification Examinations. Unsuccessful candidates who wish to be retested must reapply, submit all applicable fees and documentation, and re-establish eligibility.

Eligibility: All eligibility criteria of practice experience and/or educational preparation must be met by the time of application. It is the candidate's decision to choose the appropriate examination, based on the content outline, the individual's practice experience and NCC eligibility criteria.

Forms: All required forms must be submitted, and must include all requested information. If the forms are missing information, your application will be returned or you may be found ineligible to sit for the exam. Be sure the RN licensure information is completed. Be sure your documentation is signed by your supervisor or program director, with his/her title indicated, and the date the form is signed. Review your forms before you submit them.

Fees and Refunds: The proper fee must be submitted with your application or it will be returned.

For a current exam catalog containing current fees, terms, filing deadlines and exam dates, contact the NCC at www.nccnet.org, call (312) 951-0207 or fax at (312) 951-9475.

National Certification Corporation
PO Box 11082
Chicago, IL 60611-0082

CENTER FOR CERTIFICATION PREPARATION AND REVIEW

The Center for Certification Preparation and Review (CCPR) provides practice examinations developed by nurses and is intended to familiarize candidates with the content and feel of the real test. The CCPR practice examination identifies content areas of strength and weakness, provides examples of the type and format of questions that will appear on the examination, as well as information on how to focus additional study efforts.

The CCPR program consists of: study strategies, competency statements, content outline, 160-item examination, answer key and sample answer sheet, performance assessment grid, rationales for answers and cited references. Exams are available for inpatient obstetric, maternal newborn, neonatal intensive care and low-risk neonatal nursing, as well as neonatal nurse practitioner and women's health care nurse practitioner.

More information on ordering these practice exams can be found at www.ccprnet.org.

The National Certification Corporation (NCC), a not-for-profit organization that provides a national credentialing program for nurses, physicians and other licensed health care personnel, offers candidate guides for each of the NCC examinations. These candidate guides contain competency statements, detailed test outlines, sample questions, list of book/periodical references and all NCC policies related to the test administration process.

NCC guides are available in the following areas: inpatient obstetric, low-risk neonatal, maternal newborn and neonatal intensive care nursing, as well as neonatal nurse practitioner, telephone nursing practice, women's health care nurse practitioner, electronic fetal monitoring subspecialty examination, and menopause clinician. These guides, in addition to other information regarding testing, NCC publications and links to other organizations, are available online at www.nccnet.org.

RESOURCES FOR PRE-ADMISSION AND ACHIEVEMENT TESTS IN RN AND PN PROGRAMS

The National League for Nursing (NLN) offers a wide variety of examinations designed to aid students looking to further their education in the field of nursing. NLN pre-admission exams are reliable and valid predictors of student success in nursing programs, and NLN achievement tests allow educators to evaluate course or program objectives and to compare student performance to a national sample. The NLN also provides Diagnostic Readiness Tests, Critical Thinking and Comprehensive Nursing Achievement Exams and Acceleration Challenge Exams.

NLN exams can be ordered in paper form or e-mailed directly to you as online tests. The RN program includes tests in: basic nursing care, nursing care of children, maternity and child health nursing, nursing care of adults, psychiatric mental health and pharmacology in clinical nursing, baccalaureate achievement, physical assessment, community health nursing, comprehensive psychiatric nursing, heath and illness, anatomy and physiology, and microbiology.

NLN achievement tests also cover a PN program, which includes exams in: PN fundamentals, maternity infant, child health and adult health nursing, as well as mental health concepts and PN pharmacology.

NLN Pre-NCLEX Readiness Tests serve as practice and review for the NCLEX. Comprehensive Nursing Achievement, Critical Thinking and Diagnostic Readiness Tests are complementary to one another and help students prepare for nursing practice and to pass the NCLEX.

For in-depth information about the types of tests available, ordering, and additional NLN publications, including the NLN test catalog (available for download), visit www.nln.org.

NURSING AIDES, ORDERLIES, AND ATTENDANTS

NATURE OF WORK

Nursing aides, orderlies, and attendants perform a variety of duties to care for sick and injured people. Women usually are called aides and men generally are known as orderlies. Other job titles include <u>hospital attendant</u>, <u>nursing assistant</u>, <u>auxiliary nursing worker</u>, <u>home health aide</u>, and (in mental institutions) <u>psychiatric aide</u>.

Nursing aides and orderlies answer patients' bell calls and deliver messages, serve meals, feed patients who are unable to feed themselves, make beds, and bathe and dress patients. They also may give massages, take temperatures, and assist patients in getting out of bed and walking. Orderlies provide many of the same services. Orderlies also escort patients to operating and examining rooms and transport and set up heavy equipment. Some attendants may work in hospital pharmacies or supply rooms.

The duties of nursing aides depend on the policies of the institutions where they work, the type of patient being care for, and -- equally important -- the capacities and resourcefulness of the nursing aide or orderly. In some hospitals, they may clean patients' rooms and do other household tasks. In others, under the supervision of registered nurses and licensed practical nurses, they may assist in the care of patients. The tasks performed for patients differ considerably, and depend on whether the patient is confined to his bed following major surgery, is recovering after a disabling accident or illness, or needs assistance with daily activities because of infirmity caused by advanced age.

PLACES OF EMPLOYMENT

About 600,000 persons work as nursing aides, orderlies, and attendants; more than four-fifths are women. Most of them work in hospitals. Others work primarily in nursing homes and other institutions that provide facilities for care and recuperation. A small number give supportive services to patients in their homes.

TRAINING OTHER QUALIFICATIONS, AND ADVANCEMENT

Although some employers prefer high school graduates, many, such as Veterans Administration hospitals, hire non-graduates. Many employers accept applicants 17 or 18 years of age. Others—particularly nursing homes and mental hospitals—prefer to hire more mature men and women who are at least in their mid-twenties.

Nursing aides generally are trained after they are hired. Some institutions combine on-the-job training, under the close supervision of registered or licensed practical nurses, with classroom instruction. Students learn to take and record temperatures, bathe patients, change linens on beds that are occupied by patients, and move and lift patients. Training may last several days or a few months, depending on the policies of the hospital, the complexity of the duties and the aide's aptitude for the work. The Manpower Development and Training Act and the Vocational Education Act provide funds for many programs which train nursing aides.

Courses in home nursing and first aid, offered by many public school systems and other community agencies, provide a useful background of knowledge for the work. Volunteer work and temporary summer jobs in hospitals and similar institutions also are helpful. Applicants should be healthy, tactful, patient, understanding, emotionally stable, and dependable. Nursing aides, as other health workers, should have a genuine desire to help people, be able to work as part of a team, and be willing to accept some menial tasks.

Opportunities for promotions are limited without further training. Some acquire specialized training to prepare for better paying positions such as hospital operating room technician.

To become licensed practical nurses, nursing aides must complete the year of specialized training required for licensing. Some in-service programs allow nursing aides to get this training while they continue to work part -time.

EMPLOYMENT OUTLOOK

Employment of nursing aides is expected to increase very rapidly through the 2010s. In addition to those needed because of occupational growth, many thousands of nursing aides will be needed each year to replace workers who die, retire, or leave the occupation for other reasons.

Most jobs for nursing aides and orderlies are in hospitals, but many new openings will be in nursing homes, convalescent homes, and other long-term care facilities. Major reasons for expected occupational growth are the increasing need for medical care of a growing population, including a larger proportion of elderly people; the increasing ability of people to pay for health care; the growth of public and private health insurance plans; and the expanded medical services of Medicare and Medicaid. Employment opportunities also will arise as hospitals continue to delegate to nursing aides tasks which, although associated with patient care, do not require the training or registered and licensed practical nurses.

EARNINGS AND WORKING CONDITIONS

Nursing aides, orderlies, and attendants earned slightly less than the average for all non-supervisory workers on private payrolls, except farming. Nursing aides employed full time by nursing homes and related facilities earned considerably less than those in hospitals.

With few exceptions, the scheduled workweek of attendants in hospitals is 40-hours or less. Because nursing care must be available to patients on a 24-hour-a-day basis, scheduled hours include night work and work on weekends and holidays.

Attendants in hospitals and similar institutions generally received paid vacations which, after one year of service, may be a week or more in length. Paid holidays and sick leave, hospitalization and medical benefits, and pension plans also are available to many hospital employees.

SOURCES OF ADDITIONAL INFORMATION

Information about employment may be obtained from local hospitals and State and metropolitan health career programs.

Additional information about the work of nursing aides, orderlies, and attendants may be obtained from:

ANA Committee on Nursing Careers,

American Nurses' Association

2420 Pershing road,

Kansas City, MO. 64108

Divisions of Careers and Recruitment,

American Hospital Association,

840 North Lake Shore Drive,

Chicago, Ill. 60611.

In addition, the local office of the State employment service may be a source of information about the Manpower Development and Training Act, Vocational Education Act, and other programs that provide training opportunities.

———

NURSE'S AIDE

DUTIES

Assists physicians, nurses and other health care professionals in the care and treatment of patients; maintains personal, patient and room cleanliness; follows isolation procedures in the disposal of soiled linen, measures resident urinary output, assists patients with use of bedpan, provides perinatal (skin) care, takes oral and rectal temperature, takes radial pulse and counts respirations, gives complete bed bath, gives shower, gives back rub, provides foot, fingernail, mouth, denture care; shaves and dresses patients ; feeds dependent patients; transfers patients from bed to wheelchair; assists patients move up in bed; positions patients on side; assists patients to move and ambulate; performs related duties.

SCOPE OF THE EXAMINATION
The written test will cover knowledge, skills, and/or abilities in such areas as:
1. Fundamentals of health and nursing care;
2. Medical terminology; and
3. Understanding and interpreting written material.

HOW TO TAKE A TEST

You have studied long, hard and conscientiously.

With your official admission card in hand, and your heart pounding, you have been admitted to the examination room.

You note that there are several hundred other applicants in the examination room waiting to take the same test.

They all appear to be equally well prepared.

You know that nothing but your best effort will suffice. The "moment of truth" is at hand: you now have to demonstrate objectively, in writing, your knowledge of content and your understanding of subject matter.

You are fighting the most important battle of your life—to pass and/or score high on an examination which will determine your career and provide the economic basis for your livelihood.

What extra, special things should you know and should you do in taking the examination?

BEFORE THE TEST

YOUR PHYSICAL CONDITION IS IMPORTANT
　　　　If you are not well, you can't do your best work on tests. If you are half asleep, you can't do your best either. Here are some tips:

1) Get about the same amount of sleep you usually get. Don't stay up all night before the test, either partying or worrying—DON'T DO IT!
2) If you wear glasses, be sure to wear them when you go to take the test. This goes for hearing aids, too.
3) If you have any physical problems that may keep you from doing your best, be sure to tell the person giving the test. If you are sick or in poor health, you really cannot do your best on any test. You can always come back and take the test some other time.

AT THE TEST

EXAMINATION TECHNIQUES
1) Read the general instructions carefully. These are usually printed on the first page of the exam booklet. As a rule, these instructions refer to the timing of the examination; the fact that you should not start work until the signal and must stop work at a signal, etc. If there are any *special* instructions, such as a choice of questions to be answered, make sure that you note this instruction carefully.

2) When you are ready to start work on the examination, that is as soon as the signal has been given, read the instructions to each question booklet, underline any key words or phrases, such as *least, best, outline, describe* and the like. In this way you will tend to answer as requested rather than discover on reviewing your paper that you *listed without describing*, that you selected the *worst* choice rather than the *best* choice, etc.

3) If the examination is of the objective or multiple-choice type – that is, each question will also give a series of possible answers: A, B, C or D, and you are called upon to select the best answer and write the letter next to that answer on your answer paper – it is advisable to start answering each question in turn. There may be anywhere from 50 to 100 such questions in the three or four hours allotted and you can see how much time would be taken if you read through all the questions before beginning to answer any. Furthermore, if you come across a question or group of questions which you know would be difficult to answer, it would undoubtedly affect your handling of all the other questions.

4) If the examination is of the essay type and contains but a few questions, it is a moot point as to whether you should read all the questions before starting to answer any one. Of course, if you are given a choice – say five out of seven and the like – then it is essential to read all the questions so you can eliminate the two which are most difficult. If, however, you are asked to answer all the questions, there may be danger in trying to answer the easiest one first because you may find that you will spend too much time on it. The best technique is to answer the first question, then proceed to the second, etc.

5) Time your answers. Before the exam begins, write down the time it started, then add the time allowed for the examination and write down the time it must be completed, then divide the time available somewhat as follows:
   - If 3-1/2 hours are allowed, that would be 210 minutes. If you have 80 objective-type questions, that would be an average of 2-1/2 minutes per question. Allow yourself no more than 2 minutes per question, or a total of 160 minutes, which will permit about 50 minutes to review.
   - If for the time allotment of 210 minutes there are 7 essay questions to answer, that would average about 30 minutes a question. Give yourself only 25 minutes per question so that you have about 35 minutes to review.

6) The most important instruction is to *read each question* and make sure you know what is wanted. The second most important instruction is to *time yourself properly* so that you answer every question. The third most important instruction is to *answer every question*. Guess if you have to but include something for each question. Remember that you will receive no credit for a blank and will probably receive some credit if you write something in answer to an essay question. If you guess a letter – say "B" for a multiple-choice question – you may have guessed right. If you leave a blank as an answer to a multiple-choice question, the examiners may respect your

feelings but it will not add a point to your score. Some exams may penalize you for wrong answers, so in such cases *only*, you may not want to guess unless you have some basis for your answer.

7) Suggestions
   a. Objective-type questions
     1. Examine the question booklet for proper sequence of pages and questions
     2. Read all instructions carefully
     3. Skip any question which seems too difficult; return to it after all other questions have been answered
     4. Apportion your time properly; do not spend too much time on any single question or group of questions
     5. Note and underline key words – *all, most, fewest, least, best, worst, same, opposite,* etc.
     6. Pay particular attention to negatives
     7. Note unusual option, e.g., unduly long, short, complex, different or similar in content to the body of the question
     8. Observe the use of "hedging" words – *probably, may, most likely,* etc.
     9. Make sure that your answer is put next to the same number as the question
     10. Do not second-guess unless you have good reason to believe the second answer is definitely more correct
     11. Cross out original answer if you decide another answer is more accurate; do not erase until you are ready to hand your paper in
     12. Answer all questions; guess unless instructed otherwise
     13. Leave time for review

   b. Essay questions
     1. Read each question carefully
     2. Determine exactly what is wanted. Underline key words or phrases.
     3. Decide on outline or paragraph answer
     4. Include many different points and elements unless asked to develop any one or two points or elements
     5. Show impartiality by giving pros and cons unless directed to select one side only
     6. Make and write down any assumptions you find necessary to answer the questions
     7. Watch your English, grammar, punctuation and choice of words
     8. Time your answers; don't crowd material

8) Answering the essay question

Most essay questions can be answered by framing the specific response around several key words or ideas. Here are a few such key words or ideas:

M's: manpower, materials, methods, money, management
P's: purpose, program, policy, plan, procedure, practice, problems, pitfalls, personnel, public relations

a. Six basic steps in handling problems:
    1. Preliminary plan and background development
    2. Collect information, data and facts
    3. Analyze and interpret information, data and facts
    4. Analyze and develop solutions as well as make recommendations
    5. Prepare report and sell recommendations
    6. Install recommendations and follow up effectiveness

b. Pitfalls to avoid
    1. *Taking things for granted* – A statement of the situation does not necessarily imply that each of the elements is necessarily true; for example, a complaint may be invalid and biased so that all that can be taken for granted is that a complaint has been registered
    2. *Considering only one side of a situation* – Wherever possible, indicate several alternatives and then point out the reasons you selected the best one
    3. *Failing to indicate follow up* – Whenever your answer indicates action on your part, make certain that you will take proper follow-up action to see how successful your recommendations, procedures or actions turn out to be
    4. *Taking too long in answering any single question* – Remember to time your answers properly

EXAMINATION SECTION

EXAMINATION SECTION
TEST 1

DIRECTIONS: Each question or incomplete statement is followed by several suggested answers or completions. Select the one that BEST answers the question or completes the statement. *PRINT THE LETTER OF THE CORRECT ANSWER IN THE SPACE AT THE RIGHT.*

1. Keeping the tables and other surfaces clean in the examination room will help to break the _____ link in the chain of infection.   1.____

   A. portal of exit
   B. portal of entry
   C. mode of transmission
   D. reservoir

2. Of the following foods, _____ would typically serve as the best source of dietary fiber.   2.____

   A. kidney beans
   B. pears and apples
   C. lima beans
   D. celery

3. The identification of support resources available to a patient who wishes to enhance wellness would probably be included in the _____ stage of the nursing process.   3.____

   A. diagnosis
   B. evaluation
   C. planning
   D. implementation

4. According to the CDC, hand washing for the purpose of preventing the spread of microorganisms should be carried out for a minimum of   4.____

   A. 10 seconds
   B. 20 seconds
   C. 40 seconds
   D. 1 minute

5. _____ exercises are those that are designed to move each muscle and joint.   5.____

   A. Range of motion
   B. Rotation
   C. Isotonic
   D. Abduction

6. To establish and maintain therapeutic communication with an aphasic patient, a nurse assistant should   6.____

   A. familiarize the patient with ambient sounds
   B. ask simple questions that require "yes" or "no" answers
   C. speak slowly and enunciate clearly
   D. announce one's presence when entering the room

7. The nursing professional can make effective use of nonverbal cues to overcome

    A. a lack of understanding of cultural variations
    B. differences in values and beliefs
    C. cultural or language differences, such as mannerisms
    D. rapid information exchange with the hearing impaired

7._

8. An early sign of vitamin C deficiency is

    A. eczema
    B. bleeding gums
    C. emaciation
    D. headaches

8._

9. A patient needs to be repositioned in bed, but he is heavy. The nursing assistant is unsure about whether she can move the patient alone. The nursing assistant should

    A. seek the assistance of another nurse or nursing assistant
    B. wait until someone stronger comes on shift
    C. ask for the family's assistance
    D. move the patient as well as she is able

9._

10. During a nursing assessment of a patient's nutritional status, the _____ serves as a measure of a patient's protein reserves.

    A. mid-upper arm circumference
    B. triceps skinfold
    C. subscapular skinfold
    D. body mass index

10._

11. The _____ artery is used to measure blood pressure.

    A. brachial
    B. axillary
    C. radial
    D. ulnar

11._

12. Of the following, strong body odor would most likely associated with

    A. sexual abuse
    B. physical abuse
    C. emotional abuse
    D. neglect

12._

13. Each of the following is a tissue disease, EXCEPT

    A. Tetanus
    B. Strep throat
    C. Rheumatic fever
    D. Clostridium (gas gangrene)

13._

14. On the diabetic exchange lists, which of the following would be the equivalent of one slice   14.____
of bread?

    A. One bowl of cereal
    B. One baked potato
    C. 1/3 cup corn
    D. 1/2 glass milk

15. Which of the following illustrates the proper sequence for putting on PPE (personal pro-   15.____
tective equipment), from first to last?

    A. Mask, gloves, gown
    B. Mask, gown, gloves
    C. Gown, mask, gloves
    D. Gloves, gown, mask

16. Of the following nursing skills, _____ is most likely to be required during the pre-interac-   16.____
tion phase of the nurse-patient relationship.

    A. a relaxed attending attitude
    B. decision-making
    C. recognizing limitations and seeking assistance
    D. empathy

17. A patient and a nurse are discussing the patient's physical activity levels and how they   17.____
can be measured. Which of the following is NOT an appropriate measure of intensity?

    A. Pulse rate
    B. Talk test
    C. Rated perceived exertion (RPE) scale
    D. Perspiration amount

18. The sputum specimen comes from the   18.____

    A. lungs or bronchi
    B. pharynx
    C. nasal cavity
    D. oral cavity

19. The five stages of the nursing process, in their proper order, are   19.____

    A. Planning, Diagnosis, Assessment, Implementation and Evaluation.
    B. Planning, Diagnosis, Implementation, Assessment and Evaluation.
    C. Evaluation, Planning, Diagnosis, Implementation and Assessment.
    D. Assessment, Diagnosis, Planning, Implementation and Evaluation.

20. A patient's mail has been delivered to his room, but he hasn't noticed it. The nursing   20.____
assistant should

    A. hand him the mail and offer to help as needed
    B. open the mail and ask if he would like the contents read
    C. make sure the mail doesn't contain anything that might be upsetting
    D. open the mail and leave it on the bedside table

21. Older and incontinent patients are generally more susceptible to urinary tract infections   21.___
(UTIs), which involve the signs and symptoms of
      I.   foul-smelling urine
     II.   frequent urination
    III. painful urination
    IV. an inability to hold urine

    A. I and II
    B. I, II and IV
    C. II, III and IV
    D. I, II, III and IV

22. Which of the following is NOT a therapeutic communication technique?   22.___

    A. Offering opinions
    B. Reflecting
    C. Clarifying
    D. Stating observations

23. A nursing assistant who is making an occupied bed should   23.___

    A. raise the side rail on the unattended side
    B. place the dirty linen on the floor
    C. help the patient to sit in a chair while the bed is being made
    D. lower both side rails before removing the sheets

24. The Joint Commission on Accreditation of Healthcare Organizations (JCAHO) requires   24.___
CDC guidelines for staff who care directly for patients who are at a high risk for acquiring
infections. One of these requirements is that personnel should

    A. wear the full complement of PPE (personal protective equipment) during *every*
        patient encounter
    B. not wear artificial nails
    C. wear HEPA masks at all times
    D. not report to work if they have known contact with an infected person

25. A patient who is in restraints should have them moved and exercise his or her limbs   25.___
every

    A. 45 minutes
    B. 2 hours
    C. 6 hours
    D. 12 hours

KEY (CORRECT ANSWERS)

1.	D		11.	A
2.	A		12.	D
3.	C		13.	B
4.	B		14.	C
5.	A		15.	B
6.	B		16.	C
7.	C		17.	D
8.	B		18.	A
9.	A		19.	D
10.	A		20.	A

21.	B
22.	A
23.	A
24.	B
25.	B

———

TEST 2

DIRECTIONS: Each question or incomplete statement is followed by several suggested answers or completions. Select the one that BEST answers the question or completes the statement. *PRINT THE LETTER OF THE CORRECT ANSWER IN THE SPACE AT THE RIGHT.*

1. Among the body's nutrient reserves, _____ are most important to a person's resistance to infection.   1.___

    A. proteins
    B. carbohydrates
    C. fats
    D. vitamins

2. The CDC suggests that in order to produce health benefits, a person must engage in a level of physical activity that will allow them to expend _____ kilocalories per day.   2.___

    A. 80
    B. 150
    C. 250
    D. 400

3. In the planning phase of the nursing process for a patient at risk for pressure sore development, the major outcome is to   3.___

    A. maintain skin integrity
    B. regain intact skin
    C. regain ideal body weight
    D. demonstrate progressive wound healing

4. The Joint Commission on Accreditation of Healthcare Organizations (JCAHO) requires that the identification of patients be based on   4.___

    A. two separate identifiers for all services, not to include the patient's room number
    B. bar codes
    C. both the first and last name
    D. two nursing professionals double-checking all medications and procedures

5. A nurse must wear a gown to care for a patient in isolation. The nurse must   5.___

    A. not tie the gown, so it will be easier to remove later
    B. take the gown immediately to the dirty linen room afterward
    C. put the gown on after entering the room
    D. remove the gown before leaving the patient's room

6. A patient is recovering from a stroke, and the nursing assistant is helping the patient learn to walk again. The nursing assistant should   6.___

    A. encourage the use of a walker
    B. assist on the patient's weak side
    C. assist on the patient's strong side
    D. assist inconspicuously from behind

7. Symptoms of pneumonia include 7.____
      I.   runny nose
     II. rapid pulse
   III. painful breathing
   IV. elevated body temperature

   A. I and III
   B. II and III
   C. II, III and IV
   D. I, II, III and IV

8. Each of the following is considered to be a "lifestyle" disease, EXCEPT 8.____

   A. cancer
   B. atherosclerosis
   C. typhus
   D. osteoporosis

9. Which of the following practices illustrates proper body mechanics for one who works in a health care facility? 9.____

   A. Picking up dropped objects by bending at the waist with back and knees straightened
   B. Standing upright, with the feet flat on the floor
   C. Lifting heavy objects by bending at the waist and using the muscles of the lower back
   D. Leaning into a patient when lifting him

10. Which of the following is a correct measure of urinary output? 10.____

   A. 12 oz
   B. 250 cc
   C. 1.2pt
   D. 1 1/3 cup

11. Analysis is a feature of the _____ of the nursing process. 11.____

   A. planning
   B. assessment
   C. diagnosis
   D. evaluation

12. The correct pulse range for an older adult is _____ beats per minute. 12.____

   A. 30-50
   B. 60-100
   C. 80-120
   D. 130-180

13. A(n) _____ can be used to assess the quality of nursing care while the care is being   13.___
    given.

    A. audit
    B. quality assurance review
    C. retrospective review
    D. concurrent review

14. The best approach to use with a patient who is having difficulty communicating verbally is   14.___
    to

    A. compose an assessment in the "multiple-choice" format
    B. be patient and provide verbal and nonverbal feedback
    C. ask the patient to write out any important information
    D. fall back on clinical language that can later be legally substantiated

15. The most obvious signs of prolonged immobility are usually manifested in the _____   15.___
    system.

    A. musculoskeletal
    B. cardiovascular
    C. respiratory
    D. gastrointestinal

16. The primary sources of energy for the human body are   16.___

    A. minerals
    B. proteins
    C. carbohydrates
    D. fats

17. To provide a vegetarian patient with complete proteins, a nurse would combine in a sin-   17.___
    gle meal a portion of lentil soup and

    A. kidney beans
    B. milk
    C. whole wheat bread
    D. fish

18. Which of the following is NOT typically part of a nurse's physical fitness assessment?   18.___

    A. Skinfold measurements
    B. Joint flexibility
    C. Observing for signs of malnutrition
    D. Step test

19. A nursing assistant is using a waist restraint with a patient, under the physician's orders.   19.___
    The use of this restraint requires that the nursing assistant

    A. apply the restraint tightly enough to ensure non-movement
    B. release the restraint every couple of hours.
    C. watch closely for signs of skin irritation
    D. tie the restraint to the side rail

20. With a completely or partially immobilized patient, many nursing interventions for the respiratory system are aimed at promoting expansion of the chest and lungs. Which of the following would be most effective for this purpose?

    A.   Aerobic exercise
    B.   Frequent position changes
    C.   Isometric exercises
    D.   Physiotherapy

20._____

21. When entering the room of a patient who has tuberculosis, the nursing assistant wears a HEPA mask. The mask will protect the nursing assistant by breaking the _____ link in the chain of infection.

    A.   susceptible host
    B.   reservoir
    C.   portal of entry
    D.   portal of exit

21._____

22. When working with a hearing impaired resident, one should take care to

    A.   speak in a normal tone of voice
    B.   speak more loudly
    C.   speak very slowly
    D.   speak as little as possible

22._____

23. Cow's milk
    I.   does not need to be boiled before being fed to infants
    II.   is more easily digestible for an infant if it boiled than if it is pasteurized
    III.   must be boiled over a direct flame for 2-3 minutes in order to be considered safe
    IV.   should be pasteurized if it is going to be fed to an infant

    A.   I only
    B.   I and II
    C.   II, III and IV
    D.   III or IV

23._____

24. Of the following pathogens, the one that can have both harmful and beneficial effects is

    A.   E. coli
    B.   Giardia
    C.   Staphylococcus
    D.   Streptococcus

24._____

25. Which of the following areas will usually experience pressure when a patient is in the lateral position?

    A.   genitalia (men)
    B.   knees
    C.   ilium
    D.   vertebrae

25._____

KEY (CORRECT ANSWERS)

1.	A		11.	C
2.	B		12.	B
3.	A		13.	D
4.	A		14.	B
5.	D		15.	A
6.	B		16.	C
7.	C		17.	C
8.	C		18.	C
9.	A		19.	C
10.	B		20.	B

21.	C
22.	A
23.	C
24.	A
25.	C

TEST 3

DIRECTIONS: Each question or incomplete statement is followed by several suggested answers or completions. Select the one that BEST answers the question or completes the statement. *PRINT THE LETTER OF THE CORRECT ANSWER IN THE SPACE AT THE RIGHT.*

1. The Heimlich maneuver is used for a patient who has   1.____

   A. a fresh wound that will not stop bleeding
   B. a blocked airway
   C. ventricular fibrillation
   D. trouble falling asleep

2. Which of the following is NOT a major cause of fire in health care facilities?   2.____

   A. Paper or cloth piled in storage or patient areas
   B. Smoking by patients or staff in unauthorized areas
   C. Opening doors and windows for ventilation
   D. Faulty wiring or electrical equipment

3. Which of the following is NOT a purpose of the medical chart?   3.____

   A. Reviewing patient care
   B. Directing patient care
   C. Recording patient response to care
   D. Disseminating information about patient care

4. For a patient who has just finished bathing, a nursing assistant should wait a minimum of   4.____
   _____ before taking the blood pressure.

   A. 15 minutes   B. 30 minutes   C. 45 minutes   D. 1 hour

5. Which of the following risk factors is MOST likely to be associated with falls?   5.____

   A. Angina
   B. Peripheral vascular disease
   C. Postural (orthostatic) hypotension
   D. Ventricular fibrillation

6. Which of the following is an active strategy for health promotion?   6.____

   A. Immunization
   B. A low-fat diet
   C. Fluoridating a municipal water supply
   D. Fortifying homogenized milk with vitamin D

7. A patient and a nurse are discussing the patient's physical activity regimen. The patient   7.____
   is interested in adding some strength training to her routine. One of the benefits of
   strength training is

   A. greater aerobic capacity   B. improved flexibility
   C. lower blood pressure   D. improved balance

8. The basic nutrient required for tissue building and repair is   8.__

    A.   vitamins
    B.   carbohydrate
    C.   fats
    D.   protein

9. Generally, once a person reaches the age of _____, he or she is considered to be at   9.__
risk for falls.

    A.   45
    B.   55
    C.   65
    D.   75

10. A nursing assistant is conducting an assessment of a patient's nutritional status. The typ-   10.__
ical diet history includes each of the following, EXCEPT

    A.   height
    B.   clinical signs of nutritional status
    C.   the name of the person who usually prepares meals for patient
    D.   personal crises

11. Medical asepsis   11.__

    A.   renders an object free from all microorganisms
    B.   is primarily a reactive measure to contamination
    C.   involves handwashing before and after a medical procedure
    D.   is unrelated to personal hygiene

12. The nursing care plan   12.__
      I.   relates to the future
     II.   focuses on actions designed to solve or minimize a problem
    III.   is the product of a deliberate systematic process
    IV.   is holistic in focus

    A.   I and II
    B.   I and III
    C.   II and IV
    D.   I, I, III and IV

13. The most effective and nonintrusive way to prevent dehydration of a patient is to   13.__

    A.   install a saline drip
    B.   offer fluids frequently while the patient is awake
    C.   wake the patient frequently to offer fluids
    D.   bathe the patient frequently

14. Each of the following is an element of body mechanics, EXCEPT   14.____

    A. alignment
    B. range of motion
    C. coordination
    D. balance

15. Signs and symptoms of insulin shock include each of the following, EXCEPT   15.____

    A. nausea
    B. dry, flushed skin
    C. fruity-smelling breath
    D. irritability

16. A nurse determines that a vegan patient needs to include iron-rich foods in her diet.   16.____
Which of the following would best meet this requirement?

    A. Raisins
    B. Tuna
    C. Enriched pasta
    D. Molasses

17. One important limitation in applying Erickson's psychosocial development theory to nurs-   17.____
ing care is that it

    A. places an inordinate emphasis on sexual behaviors
    B. doesn't relate specific tasks to appropriate ages
    C. doesn't address cognitive or moral development
    D. does not consider the influences of biological factors

18. To avoid the buildup of static electricity in operating rooms, staff should avoid the use of   18.____

    A. long-sleeved gowns
    B. latex
    C. nylon
    D. spectacles

19. The planning phase of the nursing process would typically include   19.____

    A. discussing health care needs and priorities with the patient and family
    B. contacting other health resources
    C. discussing methods of implementation with the patient and family
    D. teachi ng therapies to the patient

20. Keeping a patient with a compromised immune system away from a carrier will help to   20.____
block the _____ link in the chain of infection.

    A. portal of entry
    B. causative agent
    C. susceptible host
    D. mode of transmission

21. Which of the following food combinations would most likely correct a dietary iron deficiency?

    A. Cod liver and turnip greens
    B. Egg whites and beans
    C. Milk and oysters
    D. Whole wheat and apricots

21._

22. Which of the following would NOT be an example of abuse or neglect?

    A. Leaving a patient in a soiled bed
    B. Restraining a patient according to a doctor's order
    C. Threatening to withhold meals
    D. Leaving a patient alone in a bathtub

22._

23. A patient who is at risk for pressure sores would benefit substantially from each of the following dietary supplements, EXCEPT

    A. vitamin A
    B. vitamin C
    C. calories
    D. zinc

23._

24. Parasympathetic responses to pain include

    A. nausea
    B. increased heart rate
    C. bronchial dilation
    D. dilation of pupils

24._

25. General guidelines for turning a patient in bed include
    I. spread your feet at least 3 feet apart when lifting, to avoid injury to your own back
    II. roll the patient like a log to protect her spine
    III. if the whole body cannot be rolled at once, roll the legs first, then the upper body
    IV. pull or push whenever possible, rather than lift

    A. I only
    B. I, II and IV
    C. II and III
    D. I, II, III and IV

25._

KEY (CORRECT ANSWERS)

1.	B		11.	C
2.	C		12.	D
3.	D		13.	B
4.	A		14.	B
5.	C		15.	D
6.	B		16.	A
7.	D		17.	C
8.	D		18.	C
9.	C		19.	C
10.	B		20.	C

21.	D
22.	B
23.	A
24.	A
25.	B

EXAMINATION SECTION
TEST 1

DIRECTIONS: Each question or incomplete statement is followed by several suggested answers or completions. Select the one that BEST answers the question or completes the statement. *PRINT THE LETTER OF THE CORRECT ANSWER IN THE SPACE AT THE RIGHT*

1. On a medical chart, the following phrase appears: "NPO until the return of peristalsis."
   This means the patient   1._____

   A. should eat soft foods only   B. is on a clear liquid diet
   C. is on a full liquid diet   D. is not permitted to eat or drink

2. In epidemiology, the term "common vehicle" refers to   2._____

   A. an organism that carries a disease or infection to a human
   B. a living host for a pathogen
   C. the first link in the chain of infection
   D. material that has been contaminated and can transport pathogens

3. When collecting data during the nursing process, a tertiary source of data would be   3._____

   A. the patient himself
   B. the medical record
   C. data from the patient's family and friends
   D. anecdotal observations

4. Which of the following is a disinfecting agent?   4._____

   A. Povidone iodine   B. Hibiclens
   C. Isopropyl alcohol   D. Hydrogen peroxide

5. Which of the following is most commonly the result of falls in the elderly?   5._____

   A. Vascular damage   B. Gastrointestinal bleeding
   C. Soft tissue damage   D. Hip fracture

6. Generally, it is considered appropriate for a nurse or nursing assistant to share information regarding a patient's status with   6._____
        I. the staff on the next shift
        II. close family members
        III. the patient's roommate
        IV. other staff who do not have contact with the patient

   The CORRECT answer is:
   A. I only   B. I or IV
   C. I, II or III   D. I, II, III or IV

7. Each of the following a factor that is likely to contribute to constipation, EXCEPT   7.____

    A. stress or anxiety
    B. decreased physical activity
    C. a low-roughage diet
    D. the routine use of enemas or laxatives

8. "Dangling" a patient serves to   8.____

    A. prevent foot drop
    B. give the attendant time to assume proper body mechanics before transferring
    C. acclimate him to the upright position
    D. assess orthostatic hypotension

9. A term that denotes total freedom from infection or infectious material is   9.____

    A. asepsis   B. disinfection
    C. quarantine   D. antisepsis

10. A patient has just finished a cold drink. Before taking an oral temperature, the nursing assistant should wait at least _____ minutes.   10.____

    A. 3 to 8   B. 10 to 20
    C. 30 to 45   D. 60 to 90

11. Which of the following would promote a patient's self-esteem while meeting social and mental health needs?   11.____

    A. Honest praise of the patient's accomplishments
    B. Letting the patient know that he is receiving the best care available
    C. Telling the patient that she is unique
    D. Accurate recording and reporting of observations

12. A statement of expected changes in a patient's health is called a/an   12.____

    A. objective   B. process objective
    C. outcome objective   D. goal

13. A patient has cognitive impairment and has trouble following instructions. A(n) _____ temperature should NOT be taken.   13.____

    A. tympanic (aural)   B. axillary
    C. rectal   D. oral

14. Which of the following nutrients is provided in significant quantities by eating fruits?   14.____

    A. Potassium   B. Niacin
    C. Phosphorus   D. Vitamin B

15. Nursing interventions for the completely or partially immobilized patient usually focus on

    A. achieving optimal elimination patterns
    B. restoring as much mobility as possible
    C. healing the syndrome or disease responsible for the patient's immobility
    D. preventing the hazards of immobility

15.____

16. Work practice controls in a health care setting are procedure that are designed to

    A. keep pathogens out of critical work areas
    B. achieve the repair or reprocessing of expensive protective barriers
    C. account for lost sharps
    D. reduce or eliminate the exposure to infection

16.____

17. The adaptive health model is focused primarily on the patient's

    A. stability   B. growth
    C. maturity   D. change

17.____

18. The most common method of assessing a patient's flexibility is to ask him or her to

    A. hyperextend the legs   B. perform several toe touches
    C. take a step test   D. perform two simple pull-ups

18.____

19. As an item of personal protective equipment (PPE), a mask will provide a protective barrier for about

    A. 10 minutes   B. 30 minutes
    C. 2 hours   D. 4 hours

19.____

20. The most significant sociological factor involved in community and family health is

    A. religion/spirituality   B. family size
    C. poverty   D. ethnicity

20.____

21 Which of the following is an important rule to remember when bathing a patient?

    A. Drain the tub immediately after the patient exits
    B. Allow the patient to be alone if he requests it
    C. Moisten any dry areas with bath oils
    D. Keep the call bell within reach

21.____

22. Which of the following is NOT a potential cardiovascular response to prolonged immobility?

    A. Thrombus formation   B. Venous vasodilation
    C. Postural hypertension   D. Diminished cardiac reserve

22.____

23. The basic level of the body's structure is the

    A. cell   B. organ
    C. system   D. tissue

23.____

24. In caring for a patient, a nursing assistant following Nola Fender's model of health promotion would direct her efforts toward

    A. determining the root causes of illness
    B. developing individual resources that enhance well-being
    C. assessing the strength of the patient's family
    D. limiting risk factors that impede wellness

24.____

25. A nursing assistant enters a patient's room to find him lying on the floor. The patient is conscious and responsive. The first thing the nursing assistant should do is

    A. ask the patient if he can sit on his own.
    B. check the patient for signs of injury
    C. help the patient up to a sitting position
    D. call for assistance from the supervising nurse

25.____

———————

KEY (CORRECT ANSWERS)

1.	D	11.	A
2.	D	12.	C
3.	B	13.	D
4.	C	14.	A
5.	C	15.	D
6.	A	16.	D
7.	A	17.	A
8.	C	18.	B
9.	A	19.	B
10.	B	20.	C

21.	D
22.	C
23.	A
24.	B
25.	D

————

TEST 2

DIRECTIONS: Each question or incomplete statement is followed by several suggested answers or completions. Select the one that BEST answers the question or completes the statement. *PRINT THE LETTER OF THE CORRECT ANSWER IN THE SPACE AT THE RIGHT*

1.   A family member has requested information about a patient. The most appropriate response would be to   1.____

    A.   refer the family to the supervising nurse
    B.   inform the family member about anything that is within one's scope of practice
    C.   check with the patient first to seek approval for disclosure
    D.   politely inform the family member that he is not entitled to this information

2.   When using a gait belt to move a patient, one should   2.____

    A.   tighten the belt while keeping two fingers between it and the patient's body
    B.   tighten the belt while gripping it entirely in the fist of the other hand
    C.   tighten it at the hips and then move it up to the waist
    D.   allow the patient to tighten it to a point that is comfortable

3.   When taking a patient's pulse, one observes each of the following, EXCEPT   3.____

    A.   rhythm   B.   force
    C.   rate   D.   pressure

4.   The single most effective means for preventing the spread of infection is   4.____

    A.   avoiding all contact with infected patients
    B.   strict sterilization protocols
    C.   PPE (personal protective equipment such as gowns, gloves, and masks)
    D.   handwashing

5.   Documentation is part of the _____ stage of the nursing process.   5.____

    A.   assessment   B.   planning
    C.   implementation   D.   evaluation

6.   People with sleep problems are typically characterized by each of the following, EXCEPT   6.____

    A.   listlessness   B.   disorientation
    C.   irritability   D.   altered consciousness

7.   Which of the following patient behaviors would be a sign of a partial airway blockage?   7.____

    A.   Clutching the throat   B.   No movement of the chest
    C.   Coughing   D.   An inability to speak

8. Which of the following is considered a "modifying factor" in the health promotion model?

    A. Biological traits
    B. Perceived barriers to health-promoting behaviors
    C. Definition of health
    D. Perceived ability to control health

8.____

9. A nursing assistant wants to avoid pulling a male patient's catheter during turning. The catheter should be

    A. held in both the patient's hands during turning
    B. taped to the patient's upper thigh
    C. taped to the bed frame
    D. taped to the patient's hip

9.____

10. A patient presents the following clinical signs: muscle weakness and leg cramps, anorexia, nausea, and decreased bowel sounds. Most likely, the patient is suffering from a deficiency of the _____ ion.

    A. phosphate   B. potassium
    C. calcium   D. chloride

10.____

11. Which of the following hazards is unique to long-term care facilities?

    A. Spills
    B. Fire hazards
    C. Swinging doors
    D. Medications for chronic illnesses or disorders

11.____

12. Disinfection is a process that will generally kill each of the following types of organisms, EXCEPT

    A. bacterial endospores   B. protozoans
    C. bacteria   D. viruses

12.____

13. Of the following variables, is most significant in determining a person's total energy needs.

    A age   B. physical activity
    C. immunity level   D. nutritional intake

13.____

14. Which of the following is a moist cold application?

    A. Ice collar   B. Disposable cold pack
    C. Ice bag   D. Cold compress

14.____

15. The formation of a hypothesis is an aspect of the _____ stage of the nursing process.

    A. assessment   B. planning
    C. implementation   D. evaluation

15.____

16. The correct way to remove a dirty isolation gown is to   16.____

    A. pull it off by the sleeve
    B. roll it dirty side in, away from one's body
    C. pull it over one's head
    D. let it drop to the floor and step out of it

17. A patient is a vegetarian who avoids all dairy products. Which of the following   17.____
foods would typically serve as the best source of calcium for this patient?

    A Okra   B. Rhubarb
    C. Oranges   D. Leafy greens

18. A nurse is evaluating a patient who has sustained a fall. The nursing evaluation   18.____
should include a(n)

    A. orthostatic blood pressure
    B. complete minimum data set (MDS)
    C. PET scan
    D. flexibility test

19. The presence of a _____ increases the likelihood that a disease will occur   19.____
in a particular person.

    A. risk factor   B. mutation
    C. morbidity value   D. relative risk

20. A patient's _____ temperature is generally most accurate.   20.____

    A. oral   B. tympanic (aural)
    C. rectal   D. axillary

21. Which of the following movements would be MOST likely to cause back injury?   21.____

    A. Rotation of the thoraco-lumbar spine
    B. Backward hyperextension of the spine, 20-30
    C. Lateral flexion of the quadratus lumborum
    D. Acute flexion of back with hips and knees flexed

22. At the secondary level, health problem prevention is concerned with   22.____

    A. discovering and treating existing health problems.
    B. preventing the occurrence of health problems.
    C. easing the pain of existing, terminal health problems.
    D. reducing the severity of existing health problems.

23. A nursing assistant placed clean bed linen in a patient's room, but the linen was   23.____
not used. The bed linen should be

    A. used for the patient's roommate   B. returned to the linen closet
    C. placed in the dirty linen container   D. destroyed

24. Which of the following situations does NOT specifically require the use of antimicrobial soaps for handwashing by nursing professionals?

24.____

    A. Nurseries
    B. Before invasive procedures
    C. Recovery units
    D. When known multiple resistant bacteria are present

25. A nurse and a patient are working together to plan health promotion. Which of the following would they do FIRST?

25.____

    A. Assign priorities to behavior changes
    B. Identify effective reinforcements and rewards
    C. Develop a schedule for implementing behavior changes
    D. Determine barriers to change

KEY (CORRECT ANSWERS)

1.	A		11.	D
2.	A		12.	A
3.	D		13.	B
4.	D		14.	D
5.	C		15.	A
6.	D		16.	B
7.	C		17.	D
8.	A		18.	A
9.	B		19.	A
10.	B		20.	C

21.	A
22.	A
23.	C
24.	C
25.	A

———————

TEST 3

DIRECTIONS: Each question or incomplete statement is followed by several suggested answers or completions. Select the one that BEST answers the question or completes the statement. *PRINT THE LETTER OF THE CORRECT ANSWER IN THE SPACE AT THE RIGHT.*

1. Which of the following is a safety measure for a patient who is having a seizure?   1.____

    A. Moving the patient to a safer environment
    B. Placing something soft between the patient's teeth
    C. Restraining the patient
    D. Protecting the airway

2. To prevent pressure ulcers, an immobilized patient should be repositioned   2.____

    A. hourly   B. every 2 hours
    C. every 4 hours   D. twice daily

3. Which of the following is NOT an appropriate fall prevention strategy?   3.____

    A. Monitoring patient for vital sign changes
    B. Restraining the patient
    C. Educating the patient about fall risks
    D. Safety checks for home environmental hazards

4. The level of aseptic control that destroys all pathogens is   4.____

    A. disinfection   B. sanitation
    C. decontamination   D. sterilization

5. Gloves MUST be worn when   5.____

    A. assisting in range of motion exercises
    B. giving a sponge bath
    C. performing perineal care
    D. feeding a patient

6. Of the following, a(n) _____ patient is LEAST likely to have a decubitus ulcer.   6.____

    A. incontinent   B. overweight
    C. immobile   D. post-surgical

7. Data collection and analysis are aspects of the   stage of the nursing process.   7.____

    A. assessment   B. planning
    C. diagnosis   D. evaluation

8. The state of sleep is NOT typically characterized by   8.____

    A. decreased responsiveness to external stimuli
    B. minimal or no change in the body's physiologic processes
    C. variable levels of consciousness
    D. minimal physical activity

9. The earliest sign of a pressure sore is 9.____

    A. numbness   B. clamminess
    C. swelling   D. discoloration

10. Micronutrients include 10.____

    A. fats   B. vitamins
    C. proteins   D.
    carbohydrates

11. Parasympathetic responses to pain include 11.____

    A. diaphoresis   B. variable breathing patterns
    C. pallor   D. increased pulse rate

12. Which of the following safety devices would be used to transfer a dependent patient from a bed to a chair? 12.____

    A. Quad cane   B. Gait belt
    C. Posey vest   D. EasyStand

13. Each of the following is an example of primary illness prevention, EXCEPT 13.____

    A. immunization   B. teaching breast self-examination
    C. family planning services   D. environmental sanitation

14. Patients with a one-sided weakness would use _____ for ambulation. 14.____

    A. a walker   B. a cane
    C. crutches   D. a wheelchair

15. When making strenuous movements, a partially immobilized patient tends to force expiration against a closed airway. This activity is known as 15.____

    A. the Heimlich maneuver   B. Korotkoff sounding
    C. apnea   D. the Valsalva maneuver

16. Erickson's theory of psychosocial development states that from ages one to three, the toddler's primary task is to develop 16.____

    A. trust   B. ingenuity
    C. autonomy   D. self-concept

17. Instruments that are used to invade a patient's nonsterile body sites must undergo 17.____

    A. high-level disinfection   B. sanitation
    C. decontamination   D. sterilization

18. Wheelchairs, beds, and stretchers should be locked   18.____
    A. whenever a patient is being positioned or moved
    B. when the clear possibility of a fall is evident
    C. only when requested by the patient or a family member
    D. only when the patient will be in the wheelchair, bed, or stretcher for an extended period

19. According to Maslow's hierarchy of needs, the types of needs are considered   19.____
    most basic to a person's health are

    A. physiological   B. self-esteem
    C. love and belonging   D. safety and security

20. The process of restoring a disabled patient to the highest possible level of   20.____
    functioning is known as

    A. rejuvenation   B. restoration
    C. remission   D. rehabilitation

21. As the nursing process method first came into accepted use, most practitioners'   21.____
    attention was focused on

    A. diagnosis   B. assessment
    C. evaluation   D. implementation

22. What is the term used to describe a person's ability to share or understand   22.____
    another person's feelings?

    A. Clairvoyance   B. Sympathy
    C. Empathy   D. Pity

23. Which of the following foods would NOT be included in a clear liquid diet?   23.____

    A. Sherbet   B. Hard candy
    C. Broth   D. Gelatin

24. The most commonly measured pulse is the _____ pulse.   24.____

    A. ulnar   B. brachial
    C. radial   D. carotid

25. In general, a patient at risk for impaired skin integrity should perform active   25.____
    range-of-motion exercises every

    A. hour   B. 2-3 hours
    C. 4-6 hours   D. day

KEY (CORRECT ANSWERS)

1.	D	11.	B
2.	B	12.	B
3.	B	13.	B
4.	D	14.	B
5.	C	15.	D
6.	D	16.	C
7.	A	17.	A
8.	B	18.	A
9.	D	19.	A
10.	B	20.	D

21.	B
22.	C
23.	A
24.	C
25.	B

———————

EXAMINATION SECTION
TEST 1

DIRECTIONS: Each question or incomplete statement is followed by several suggested answers or completions. Select the one that BEST answers the question or completes the statement. *PRINT THE LETTER OF THE CORRECT ANSWER IN THE SPACE AT THE RIGHT.*

1. The most important natural barrier that helps people to prevent the entry of pathogens is   1._____

   A. mucus
   B. T cells
   C. cilia
   D. the skin

2. A patient has right-sided weakness. When dressing the patient in a blouse, the nursing assistant should   2._____

   A. put it on the right side first
   B. put it on the left side first
   C. pull it over the head and put both arms through at once
   D. put the right arm in a sling

3. Of the following, the activity most likely to be considered a secondary-prevention activity would be   3._____

   A. immunization
   B. preventing complications
   C. enhancing rehabilitation
   D. screening

4. Which of the following activities would generally burn the most kilo-calories per hour?   4._____

   A. Cross-country skiing
   B. Bicycling
   C. Canoeing
   D. Swimming

5. Which of the following is considered to be a kind of restraint?   5._____

   A. Gait belt
   B. Abductor wedge
   C. Posey vest
   D. Cannula

6. A patient has redness and clear drainage from her right eye. The medical abbreviation for right eye is   6._____

   A. O.D.
   B. R.E.
   C. O.S.
   D. E.R.

7. A nursing assistant has stored a disinfected batch of equipment in the supply closet. The disinfection would be invalidated by   7._

    A. removing the equipment for use in another unit
    B. damage or water penetration of the packaging
    C. the movement of the equipment to another location in supply
    D. removing prepackaged items with ungloved hands

8. Direct nursing care is an element of the_____ stage of the nursing process.   8._

    A. implementation
    B. assessment
    C. diagnosis
    D. evaluation

9. Vital signs include   9._
    I. weight
    II. body temperature
    III. pulse rate
    IV. respiratory rate

    A. I and II
    B. I, II and III
    C. II, III and IV
    D. I, II, III and IV

10. A patient"s diet is found to be thiamin-deficient. Which of the following dietary elements would serve as the best remedy?   10._

    A. Fruit
    B. Bread or cereal
    C. Beans
    D. Dairy products

11. Which of the following is NOT typically a physiological manifestation of stress?   11._

    A. Pale skin
    B. Decreased urinary output
    C. Decreased blood sugar
    D. Dry mouth

12. A nursing assistant is preparing a patient for ambulation. Which of the following precautions is appropriate?   12._

    A. Dressing the patient in clothing of his or her choosing
    B. Ensuring that the patient is not dizzy or disoriented
    C. Placing a towel over any spills on the floor
    D. Checking to see if the patient can stand alone before offering assistance

13. In the nursing process,_____ are stated goals for health care activities that can be used   13.____
to plan and evaluate care.

    A. quality assurances
    B. audits
    C. standards of care
    D. criteria

14. A patient diagnosed with chronic pain may exhibit the defining characteristic of   14.____

    A. communication of pain descriptors
    B. altered muscle tone
    C. physical and social withdrawal
    D. guarded, protective behavior

15. The purpose of a turning sheet is to   15.____

    A. substitute for another person if nobody is available to move a helpless or heavy
       patient
    B. reduce friction when moving helpless or heavy patients
    C. serve as a light restraint while the patient's bed is being changed
    D. relieve pressure while supporting the patient's body

16. Of following patient positions, which typically promotes maximal chest expansion?   16.____

    A. Orthopneic
    B. Sims'
    C. Trendelenburg
    D. High Fowler's

17. Range of motion exercises can help   17.____
      I. increase aerobic capacity
     II. prevent contractures
    III. increase muscular strength
    IV. improve circulation

    A. I and II
    B. I and IV
    C. II, III and IV
    D. I, II, III and IV

18. _____ infections are associated with the delivery of health care services in a health   18.____
care facility.

    A. Vector
    B. Nosocomial
    C. Exogenous
    D. Complementary

19. Each of the following is an appropriate action to take in caring for a patient with cancer, EXCEPT

    A. keeping the patient's skin clean, dry and pressure-free
    B. using surgical asepsis for infection control
    C. remaining positive and listening to the patient's concerns
    D. providing emotional support after hair loss

19.__

20. The FIRST stage of the nursing process is

    A. planning
    B. evaluation
    C. diagnosis
    D. assessment

20.__

21. Each of the following is typically involved in the nutritional assessment of a patient, EXCEPT

    A. measuring mid-upper arm circumference
    B. comparing weight to body build
    C. girth measurements
    D. a dietary history

21.__

22. Of the stages involved in death outlined by Elizabeth Kubler Ross, the last is usually

    A. acceptance
    B. depression
    C. denial
    D. anger

22.__

23. Of the following foods,_____ would most effectively boost the vitamin B content of a patient's diet.

    A. fruits
    B. dairy products
    C. simple sugars
    D. poultry

23.__

24. When changing unsterile dressing, the nursing assistant should wash hands
    I. before the procedure
    II. after removing the soiled dressing
    III. after the completion of the procedure

    A. I only
    B. II only
    C. II and III
    D. I, II and III

24.__

25. Which of the following would be a care consideration for maintaining the comfort of an elderly patient?   25.____

    A. Ensuing privacy
    B. Maintaining the patient's body temperature at a level that is agreeable
    C. Teaching about facility policies and procedures
    D. Allowing familiar caregivers access to the patient

KEY (CORRECT ANSWERS)

1.	D		11.	C
2.	A		12.	B
3.	D		13.	C
4.	A		14.	C
5.	C		15.	B
6.	A		16.	A
7.	B		17.	C
8.	A		18.	B
9.	C		19.	B
10.	B		20.	D

21.	C
22.	A
23.	D
24.	D
25.	B

TEST 2

DIRECTIONS: Each question or incomplete statement is followed by several suggested answers or completions. Select the one that BEST answers the question or completes the statement. *PRINT THE LETTER OF THE CORRECT ANSWER IN THE SPACE AT THE RIGHT.*

1. Which of the following positions is used specifically to relax tension of the patient's abdominal muscles?   1.__

   A. Knee-chest
   B. Trendelenburg
   C. Sim's
   D. Fowler's

2. Approximately_____ percent of an average American's energy intake is derived from carbohydrates.   2.__

   A. 15
   B. 45
   C. 65
   D. 80

3. When caring for a patient with a Foley catheter, it is important to   3.__

   A. remove the catheter for frequent inspection
   B. attach the drainage bag to the side rail of the bed
   C. empty the drainage bag at the beginning of every shift
   D. keep the drainage bag below the bladder

4. The Joint Commission on Accreditation of Healthcare Organizations (JCAHO) requires that, in order to reduce the risk of falls, health care facilities such as hospitals should   4.__

   A. avoid prescribing medications that may contribute to falls
   B. educate patients about the dangers inherent in many medications
   C. establish a fall-reduction program and evaluate its effectiveness
   D. restrain patients who are at a high risk for falling

5. Macronutrients include each of the following, EXCEPT   5.__

   A. carbohydrates
   B. fats
   C. proteins
   D. minerals

6. A person's body temperature is   6._____
    I.   lowest in the morning
    II. higher during infection in older patients than in younger pa tients
    III. highest in the afternoon or evening
    IV. most appropriately measured with a glass thermometer

    A. I only
    B. I and III
    C. II, III and IV
    D. I, II, III and IV

7. A patient who is at risk for pressure sores should have a systematic skin inspection at   7._____
least

    A. every 4 hours
    B. twice daily
    C. daily
    D. every 2 days

8. A patient has experienced some hearing loss. In order to communicate clearly with the   8._____
patient, a nurse should

    A. speak while looking directly at the patient
    B. use simple hand gestures
    C. speaking loudly and slowly
    D. speak in a higher pitch than normal

9. A nursing assistant is teaching a patient how to perform range-of-motion exercises inde-   9._____
pendently. He should instruct the patient to do each of the following, EXCEPT

    A. perform each exercise to the point of slight resistance
    B. perform each exercise three times
    C. vary the sequence of the exercises from day to day
    D. perform each series of exercises twice daily

10. Which of the following is a method of cleaning equipment with chemicals or boiling   10._____
water?

    A. Sterilization
    B. Disinfection
    C. Decontamination
    D. Antisepsis

11. The best explanation for the relatively higher incidence of obesity in low-income commu-   11._____
nities is related to

    A. the food preferences of cultural or ethnic groups who predominate these popula-
tions
    B. a tendency to purchase greater amounts of pre-processed foods
    C. a greater reliance on daily products
    D. a reliance on cheaper cuts of meat

12. The following steps to turning a patient from his back to his side in bed, in their proper order, are

    I.   With your back straight and knees bent, pull the person toward you.
    II. Put both of your arms under the patient's waist and hips. Pull the hips toward you so the buttocks stick out a little.
    III. Put one arm under the patient's hips and the other under his up per back
    IV. Gently push to lift the hip and shoulder off the bed until the patient is resting on the hip and shoulder farthest from you.

    A. I, II, III, IV
    B. II, IV, III, I
    C. III, I, IV, II
    D. III, IV, I, II

12._

13. A nurse is assessing a patient's ability to achieve wellness, applying the model of health promotion developed by Nola Pender. Which of the following would be considered a modifying factor involved in the patient's ability to participate in health-promoting behavior?

    A. The influence of the patient's family
    B. The patient's perceived level of control over his or her health
    C. The barriers that the patient perceives to health-promoting behavior
    D. The overall importance of health to the patient

13._

14. The development of goals and objectives is an aspect of the _____ stage of the nursing process.

    A. assessment
    B. planning
    C. implementation
    D. evaluation

14._

15. A patient is unresponsive. How many initial breaths should be administered before checking the pulse?

    A. 2
    B. 3
    C. 4
    D. 6

15._

16. A patient is dying. The last sensory input she will lose will be her

    A. taste
    B. smell
    C. sight
    D. hearing

16._

17. _____ precautions require the use of personal protective equipment within 3 feet of the   17._____
patient

    A. Enteric
    B. Droplet
    C. Airborne
    D. Contact

18. Which of the following is the term for a sheet that is placed crosswise over the bottom   18._____
sheet in the middle of a bed?

    A. Turning sheet
    B. Top sheet
    C. Drawsheet
    D. Transfer sheet

19. When transferring a patient, most of the patient's weight should be supported by the   19._____
nursing assistant's

    A. shoulders
    B. upper arms
    C. legs
    D. back

20. A vaccination is an example of_____ health problem prevention.   20._____

    A. primary
    B. secondary
    C. tertiary
    D. prophylactic

21. A patient and a nurse are discussing the possibility of beginning a routine of moderate   21._____
physical activity. The patient, who has been inactive for a long time, is concerned about
the possibility of adverse effects. The most common adverse effect of physical activity is

    A. dizziness and anxiety
    B. cardiac arrest
    C. chronic fatigue
    D. musculoskeletal injury

22. If the diet of a child relies excessively on milk, the child is most at risk for a(n) _____   22._____
deficiency.

    A. calcium
    B. vitamin A
    C. vitamin D
    D. iron

23. When cleaning and disinfecting objects, nursing professionals should be led by each of the following guidelines, EXCEPT

    A. for the initial rinse, use hot water
    B. wash with hot water and soap
    C. for the final rinse, use warm water
    D. use an abrasive to clean equipment with grooves and corners

23.___

24. When treating a patient with pressure sores, the head of the bed should be elevated to a maximum angle of_____ degrees.

    A. 5
    B. 15
    C. 30
    D. 45

24.___

25. If a patient is isolated under enteric precautions, the purpose is usually to prevent

    A. infections transmitted by direct or indirect contact with infected blood or serae
    B. infections transmitted through direct or indirect contact with feces
    C. highly transmissible infections not requiring strict isolation but spread by close or direct contact
    D. stomach upset

25.___

———

KEY (CORRECT ANSWERS)

1.	D		11.	B
2.	B		12.	C
3.	D		13.	A
4.	C		14.	B
5.	D		15.	A
6.	B		16.	D
7.	C		17.	B
8.	A		18.	C
9.	C		19.	C
10.	B		20.	A

21.	D
22.	D
23.	A
24.	C
25.	B

———

TEST 3

DIRECTIONS: Each question or incomplete statement is followed by several suggested answers or completions. Select the one that BEST answers the question or completes the statement. *PRINT THE LETTER OF THE CORRECT ANSWER IN THE SPACE AT THE RIGHT.*

1. The phrase "fifth vital sign" usually refers to

    A. blood glucose
    B. emotional distress
    C. functional status
    D. pain

1._____

2. Falls among elderly patients most commonly occur during activities that

    A. require physical dexterity
    B. are part of the person's daily routine
    C. involve high aerobic demands
    D. are risky and beyond the person's capabilities

2._____

3. A physician asks the nursing assistant to place a patient in the Sims' position. The patient should be

    A. in a semi-upright sitting position with the knees bent
    B. flat on the back with the head lower than the pelvis
    C. on her left side, left leg extended and right leg flexed
    D. in a kneeling position, supported by the knees and the shoulders, with the chest sagging down

3._____

4. Protective gloves should be used

    A. whenever one is within three feet of a patient
    B. only when directly handling specimens
    C. when there is actual, observable contact with blood or body fluids
    D. any time one is likely to touch a patient

4._____

5. The most common infecting organism associated with nosocomial infections is

    A. Enterococcus
    B. Staphylococcus aureus
    C. Lactobacillus
    D. E. coli

5._____

6. Each of the following is an important priority of data collection during the assessment stage of the nursing process, EXCEPT

    A. communicating with the patient, rather than consulting secondary sources
    B. including information about both strengths and needs
    C. arranging results in a way that is easily retrievable by future researchers
    D. including the patient's responses to current alterations

6._____

7. Signs of cerebrovascular problems include

    I.   numbness
    II. blurred vision
    III. dizziness
    IV. shortness of breath

    A. I and II
    B. I, II, and III
    C. II and IV
    D. I, II, III and IV

7.___

8. The primary, secondary and tertiary levels of preventive action are elements of the_____ phase of the nursing process.

    A. assessment
    B. planning
    C. intervention
    D. evaluation

8.___

9. A patient is upset and crying about the recent death of his spouse. The most appropriate response to this would be to

    A. point out all the good things the patient can appreciate in his life
    B. leave the patient alone in his grief
    C. suggest some activities that might help the patient take his mind off things
    D. sit with the patient and allow him to talk about his feelings if he wishes

9.___

10. The performance of the Heinilich maneuver requires placement of the thumb

    A. just below the navel
    B. just above the navel
    C. right below the lower end of the sternum
    D. in the center of the sternum

10.___

11. A patient's dietary orders require that he receive a certain number of milliliters of juice. The container is a four ounce container. In order to determine the number of milliliters in the container, the nursing assistant should

    A. divide 30 by 4
    B. divide 60 by 4
    C. multiply 4 by 30
    D. multiply 4 by 60

11.___

12. A nursing assistant is putting a patient to bed for the night. Which of the following would NOT be a safety measure that should be taken?

    A. Using side rails
    B. Providing long intravenous tubing
    C. Using night-lights
    D. Placing the bed in a high position

12.___

13. At the primary level, health problem prevention is concerned with   13.____

    A. preventing the occurrence of health problems.
    B. discovering and treating existing health problems.
    C. easing the pain of existing, terminal health problems.
    D. reducing the severity of existing health problems.

14. "Nutrition" is most accurately defined as   14.____

    A. the kinds of food that a person habitually eats
    B. the sum of all the interactions between a person and the food he or she consumes
    C. the assimilation of food, through the stomach and bowels, into the body's organ systems
    D. the biochemical and physiologic processes by which the body grows and maintains itself

15. A nurse attempts to meet patient needs by applying Maslow's hierarchy to nursing care. In doing this, it is important for the health care professional to remember that the   15.____

    A. professional must always take modifying factors into account
    B. care should always focus on the patient's current needs, rather than strict adherence to the theoretical hierarchy
    C. hierarchy is not typically relevant to tertiary care
    D. patient's self-esteem needs must never be given priority over physiological needs

16. OSHA recommends that hypodermic needles should not be recapped if it can be avoided; however, if it is necessary, recapping should be performed using   16.____

    A. both hands
    B. at least one other person
    C. the one-handed "scoop" method
    D. puncture-proof gloves

17. Piaget's theory of cognitive development may be helpful to nurses in health promotion, in that it can help nurses to   17.____

    A. understand how children of various ages interpret health and health care
    B. identify the basic physical and psychosocial needs of children
    C. provide a basis for the assessment of a child's moral code
    D. provide a patient with tools to crisis-coping tools

18. To be sure that he is measuring a patient's weight accurately, a nursing assistant should weigh the patient   18.____

    A. at a different time each day
    B. after a meal
    C. after a nap
    D. at the same time every day

19. A patient and a nurse are discussing the patient's physical activity regimen. The patient wonders when would be the best time to perform stretching exercises. In order to increase flexibility, the best time to stretch is

    A. during moderate physical activity
    B. when checking the pulse
    C. during the post-exercise cool-down
    D. about an hour before exercising

19._

20. The nursing assessment of a patient's nutritional status typically involves a dietary history of the patient's previous

    A. 24 hours
    B. 3 days
    C. week
    D. 2 weeks

20._

21. A patient is deaf. The best way to communicate with her would be to

    A. use simple hand gestures
    B. speak loudly
    C. write out information
    D. speak slowly to allow for lip-reading

21._

22. A nursing assistant is helping an immobilized patient to perform passive range-of-motion exercises. Which of the following would NOT be a guideline for this procedure?

    A. If contracture is present, the exercises should be stopped immediately.
    B. Body parts should be moved slowly. Move the body parts slowly
    C. Only the limb being exercised should be exposed.
    D. If rigidity occurs, pressure should be applied against the rigidity and the exercise slowly continued.

22._

23. A nursing assistant has become annoyed with a patient's extreme depression and negativity, and is having a hard time viewing him objectively. In this situation, the most appropriate action would be to

    A. gently suggest that there are other patients in the same unit whose situations are more difficult
    B. excuse oneself and calm down outside the room, if doing so poses no risk to the patient
    C. confront the patient about the unhelpfulness of his attitude
    D. remind the patient that emotions and attitude can have a direct effect on one's health

23._

24. The nursing history of an assessment that is concerned with infection risk will typically involve questioning the patient about each of the following, EXCEPT

    A. physical activity
    B. urinary frequency or difficulty
    C. appetite
    D. nausea

24._

25. The CDC, to encourage greater participation in physical activity, recommends that peo-   25._____
    ple engage in a minimum of

    A. 60 minutes of high-intensity physical activity at least 3 days a week
    B. 60 minutes of moderate-intensity physical activity on most days of the week
    C. 30 minutes of moderate-intensity physical activity on most days of the week
    D. 30 minutes of light-intensity physical activity every day

---

KEY (CORRECT ANSWERS)

1.	D		11.	C
2.	B		12.	D
3.	C		13.	A
4.	C		14.	B
5.	D		15.	B
6.	C		16.	C
7.	B		17.	A
8.	B		18.	D
9.	D		19.	C
10.	B		20.	A

21.	C
22.	A
23.	B
24.	A
25.	C

EXAMINATION SECTION
TEST 1

DIRECTIONS: Each question or incomplete statement is followed by several suggested
answers or completions. Select the one that BEST answers the question or
completes the statement. *PRINT THE LETTER OF THE CORRECT ANSWER
IN THE SPACE AT THE RIGHT.*

1. Assume that you are assigned to a health center. A middle-aged man walks in and says   1.____
that he doesn't feel well. He complains of a slight pain in the chest and has difficulty
breathing.
Of the following actions, the one you should take is to

    A.   isolate him immediately as he may have *Asian flu*
    B.   find out what he has eaten as he may have food poisoning
    C.   ask him to sit down and see if he can catch his breath
    D.   see that he is seated and then call a doctor

2. A baby who has been brought to the health center for an examination has been crying   2.____
continuously for 20 minutes. The BEST of the following actions you should take is to

    A.   have the baby examined by the first available physician
    B.   ask the others who are waiting if they would object to the baby being examined out
of turn
    C.   call the situation to the attention of the nurse in charge
    D.   do nothing as there are probably others who are ill and need to see the doctor

3. Suppose that a mother comes into the health center, carrying a 3-year-old child who is ill.   3.____
The mother tells you that the child has a temperature of 102°F, his nose is stuffed, and
he is sneezing.
For you to seat the mother and child apart from the others who are waiting for the physician is

    A.   *correct;* the other children and adults in the clinic should not be exposed to a dis-
ease which may be contagious
    B.   *incorrect;* the mother might be offended if she were treated differently than the
other patients
    C.   *correct;* the nurse is in a good position to diagnose patients when the doctor is not
available
    D.   *incorrect;* you should wait until the physician makes his diagnosis before isolating
the child

4. In the performance of her work, it is not enough that the employee be alert to the imme-   4.____
diate demands of her own job; she must be constantly aware of the basic function of the
clinic.
This statement means that a worker should view the ultimate purpose of her job as

    A.   giving effective service to patients
    B.   getting the most work done in the shortest time
    C.   following to the letter all orders given to her
    D.   reporting punctually and working diligently

5. While serving at an eye clinic, you are instructed to answer the phone by saying, *Eye*   5.___
   Clinic, Miss Jones speaking.
   Of the following, the BEST reason for this practice is that

   A. it sets the tone for a brief, concise telephone conversation
   B. it is the standard practice recommended by the telephone company and is familiar
       to callers
   C. the caller will understand that he cannot ask for medical information, since you are
       not a physician
   D. the caller will know whether he is speaking to the person he wants to reach

6. If a telephone call is received for a doctor while he is examining a patient, it would be   6.___
   BEST to

   A. tell the caller to telephone again when the doctor can receive a call
   B. take the caller's telephone number and have the doctor return the call when he is
       free
   C. ask the nature of the call in order to determine if it requires the doctor's immediate
       attention
   D. refer the call to the nurse in charge as she may have the information the caller
       requires

7. Suppose that a patient who attends the clinic has made frequent complaints, usually   7.___
   unjustified.
   Of the following, the BEST reason for not ignoring another complaint from her is that

   A. she is likely to take her complaint to a higher level
   B. even though past complaints have been unjustified, this particular one may require
       attention
   C. a patient is often pacified if you pretend that you will look into her complaint
   D. no distinction should be made in your attitude toward patients

8. Clinic appointments are less likely to be broken if you   8.___

   A. make appointments on dates which are convenient for the patients
   B. stress to each patient that a broken appointment inconveniences other patients
   C. threaten not to make any more appointments for patients who break appointments
       without a good reason
   D. arrange the schedule of appointments so that patients do not have to wait in the
       clinic

9. Assume that every day the schedule of the clinic is severely disrupted because several   9.___
   patients without appointments must be treated for emergency conditions. Of the following, the BEST suggestion you could make in order to minimize disruption is that

   A. one morning a week be set aside when all emergency cases will be treated
   B. applicants who claim emergency conditions be screened to see which of them
       really need emergency treatment
   C. unassigned periods be allowed in the schedule in anticipation of emergency cases
   D. the clinic be kept open each evening until all patients have been treated

10. Suppose that a woman who is scheduled to appear at 3:30 P.M. comes into the clinic at 10 A.M. and says she is ill and must see the doctor at once. The clinic is already quite crowded.
It would be BEST for you to

    A. try to determine if she is really ill, since some patients use the claim as a ruse to get prompt attention
    B. tell her to return at the proper time, since the other patients will become disorderly if others are taken before they are
    C. see if the head nurse will take her out of turn, since she may need prompt care
    D. see if a clinic physician is willing to see her, since public reaction would be hostile if the condition of the woman became worse while waiting

10.____

11. Some authorities advocate that the mother not stay in the same room when a child of 3 or 4 is being treated by the doctor.
Of the following, the BEST reason for this is that the

    A. mother might become upset if she watches the treatment
    B. child is less likely to accept the doctor's authority
    C. mother will prolong the examination by questioning the doctor about her child
    D. child will mature more rapidly if he is not always accompanied by his mother

11.____

12. Assume that a patient tells you that he is not going to follow the treatment recommended by the physician because he doesn't have long to live anyway.
It would be BEST for you to

    A. report the conversation to the physician
    B. point out to the patient that it is foolish to come for treatment if he will not follow the recommendations given him by the physician
    C. explain to the patient that he will live longer and less painfully if he follows the physician's recommendations
    D. try to get a relative in whom the patient has confidence to persuade him to follow the physician's recommendations

12.____

13. Suppose that a patient who has just received treatment in the clinic complains loudly that she was kept waiting a lone time and then received hasty and inadequate treatment.
It is BEST for you to

    A. explain that treatment is necessarily hasty because the clinic is busy
    B. avoid arguing with her, since ill people are often overwrought
    C. tell her she is not qualified to decide whether treatment is adequate
    D. refer the patient back to the physician for completion of treatment

13.____

14. Assume that a patient who has been coming to the clinic for some time asks you, *Do I have a heart condition?* You know that his clinic record card bears the notation *heart murmur.*
Under these circumstances, it would be BEST for you to tell him

    A. he has a heart murmur, since he obviously knows this and his card gives you the information
    B. he does not have a heart condition, since the doctor would have informed the patient if he wanted him to know about it

14.____

C. not to worry about it since lots of people have a heart condition
D. to ask the physician whom he has been seeing in the clinic about this

15. If a 3-year-old child refuses to stay on a scale long enough to be weighed, the BEST of   15.___
the following actions for you to take is to

    A. obtain the child's weight by first weighing the mother holding the child in her arms, and then weighing the mother alone
    B. insist that the child be weighed so that the other children in the clinic will cooperate when being weighed
    C. ask one of the special officers to assist her in weighing the child
    D. note on the record that the child refused to be weighed and let the physician determine if it is necessary to weigh the child

16. You have been asked to hand the sterile instruments to the physician while he is chang-   16.___
ing a dressing. Suppose that halfway through the procedure, the doctor drops the forceps he is using.
Of the following actions, the one that you should take at this time is to

    A. pick up the forceps with your hand and ask the doctor if he will need it any more
    B. pick up the forceps with your hand and place it with other contaminated instruments
    C. move the forceps out of the way with your foot
    D. use sterile forceps from the cabinet to pick up the forceps from the floor

17. You have been asked to prepare a list of supplies to be reordered for your clinic.   17.___
In order for you to determine how much of any item to reorder, it would be MOST important to know

    A. the average amount of the item used in a given period of time
    B. what the item is used for in the clinic
    C. how much storage space is available for these supplies
    D. the cost of each item

18. Assume that when you open a cabinet in which disinfectants are kept, you find that one   18.___
of the bottles has no label. However, there is a label on the shelf near the bottle.
Of the following, the BEST action for you to take is to

    A. paste the label on the bottle since it obviously is the label for that bottle
    B. paste the label on the bottle only if the label has the word *disinfectant* clearly marked on it
    C. place the bottle back in the cabinet and ask the nurse in charge what to do
    D. pour the contents of the bottle into the sink, rinse the bottle, and place it in the proper receptacle

19. After washing and rinsing rubber hot water bottles, hang then upside down with their   19.___
mouths open. When they are thoroughly dry, inflate them, place the stoppers into the mouths of the bottles, and leave them hanging. If they are to be stored, leave them inflated and place gauze or crushed paper between them.
On the basis of this paragraph, the one of the following statements that is MOST accurate is that, when storing hot water bottles,

A. they should be stuffed with paper
B. a free flow of air must circulate around them
C. care must be taken to prevent their sides from sticking together
D. they should be placed upside down with their mouths open

20. In filing, a cross index should be used for a record which   20.____

    A. may be filed in either of two places
    B. has been temporarily removed from the file
    C. concerns a patient who is no longer coming to the clinic
    D. will be used to remind patients of appointments

21. Assume that the cards of patients are kept in alphabetical order. You are given an alpha-   21.____
betical list of persons who have received injections for *Asian flu* at the clinic, and are
asked to see if there is a card in the file for each person on the list.
It would be BEST for you to

    A. determine if the number of cards and the number of names on the list are the same
    B. place a check mark next to each name on the list for which there is a corresponding card
    C. place a check mark on each card for which there is a corresponding name on the list
    D. prepare a second list of all cards in the file and place a check mark next to each name for which there is a corresponding name on the first list

22. Assume that there are several clinics within a health center. Patients' cards are filed   22.____
according to the clinic which they attend, and within each clinic are filed alphabetically.
Every Friday you are responsible for filing the cards of all patients who were in the health
center during that week. The cards are in mixed order.
Of the following, the FIRST step to take is to

    A. arrange the patients' cards in alphabetical order
    B. separate the cards of those patients who attended more than one clinic from all the others
    C. arrange the patients' cards according to the clinic attended
    D. arrange the patients' cards according to the date the patient attended the clinic

23. Suppose that, in Clinic A, a medical history card is prepared for each new patient. In this   23.____
clinic, a blood test is made for each patient as a routine procedure. You have been
instructed to make out either a blue card for a negative report, or a white card for a positive report, when the laboratory reports of the blood tests are received.
In order to make sure that all reports on the blood tests have been received, you
should compare the number of reports received with the number of _____ cards.

    A. medical history   B. blue
    C. white   D. blue and white

24. Assume that you are in charge of ordering supplies needed for the clinic. When reorder-   24.____
ing items, it is BEST to

    A.   count supplies at the beginning of each month and reorder an item as soon as there is no more of it in stock

    B.   determine beforehand the amount of each item which it is necessary to have on hand and reorder the item when the supply falls to this level

    C.   reorder each item in sufficient quantity to last half a year so that there will be no danger of running out of supplies

    D.   reorder all items at the beginning of each month so that no item needed will be forgotten

25.   It is usually recommended that, when new supplies of any item are received, they be placed beneath or behind supplies of the item already in stock.
Of the following, the BEST reason for this is that this procedure   25.__

    A.   requires less frequent handling of supplies
    B.   makes it easier to tell how much of each item you have on hand
    C.   allows you to use the storage space most effectively
    D.   makes it more likely that the older supplies will be used first

26.   The abbreviation *EEG* refers to a(n)   26.__

    A.   examination of the eyes and ears
    B.   inflammatory disease of the urinogenital tract
    C.   disease of the esophageal structure
    D.   examination of the brain

27.   The complete destruction of all forms of living microorganisms is called   27.__

    A.   decontamination   B.   fumigation
    C.   sterilization   D.   germination

28.   A rectal thermometer differs from other fever thermometers in that it has a   28.__

    A.   longer stem   B.   thinner stem
    C.   stubby bulb at one end   D.   slender bulb at one end

29.   The one of the following pieces of equipment which is usually used together with a sphygmometer is a   29.__

    A.   stethoscope   B.   watch
    C.   fever thermometer   D.   hypodermic syringe

30.   A curette is a   30.__

    A.   healing drug   B.   curved scalpel
    C.   long hypodermic needle   D.   scraping instrument

31.   The otoscope is used to examine the patient's   31.__

    A.   eyes   B.   ears   C.   mouth   D.   lungs

32.   A catheter is used   32.__

    A.   to close wounds
    B.   for withdrawing fluid from a body cavity
    C.   to remove cataracts
    D.   as a cathartic

33. Of the following pieces of equipment, the one that is required for making a scratch test is   33.____
    a

    A. needle   B. scalpel
    C. capillary tube   D. tourniquet

34. A hemostat is an instrument which is used to   34.____

    A. hold a sterile needle
    B. clamp off a blood vessel
    C. regulate the temperature of a sterilizer
    D. measure oxygen intake

35. Of the following medical supplies, the one that MUST be stored in a tightly sealed bottle   35.____
    is

    A. sodium fluoride
    B. alum
    C. oil of cloves
    D. aromatic spirits of ammonia

36. A person who has been exposed to an infectious disease is called   36.____

    A. a contact   B. an incubator
    C. diseased   D. infected

37. A myocardial infarct would occur in the   37.____

    A. heart   B. kidneys   C. lungs   D. spleen

38. The abbreviations *WBC* and *RBC* refer to the results of tests of the   38.____

    A. basal metabolism   B. blood
    C. blood pressure   D. bony structure

39. When a person's blood pressure is noted as 120/80, it means that his _____ blood   39.____
    pressure is _____.

    A. pulse; 120   B. pulse; 80
    C. systolic; 120   D. systolic; 80

40. The anatomical structure that contains the tonsils and adenoids is the   40.____

    A. pharynx   B. larynx   C. trachea   D. sinuses

41. An abscess can BEST be described as a   41.____

    A. loss of sensation
    B. painful tooth
    C. ruptured membrane
    D. localized formation of pus

42. Nephritis is a disease affecting the   42.____

    A. gall bladder   B. larynx
    C. kidney   D. large intestine

43. Hemoglobin is contained in the 43.___

    A. white blood cells   B. lymph fluids
    C. platelets   D. red blood cells

44. Bile is a body fluid that is MOST directly concerned with 44.___

    A. digestion   B. excretion
    C. reproduction   D. metabolism

45. Of the following bones, the one which is located below the waist is the 45.___

    A. sternum   B. clavicle   C. tibia   D. humerus

46. The one of the following which is NOT part of the digestive canal is the 46.___

    A. esophagus   B. larynx   C. duodenum   D. colon

47. The thyroid and the pituitary are part of the _____ system. 47.___

    A. digestive   B. endocrine
    C. respiratory   D. excretory

48. The one of the following which would be included in a *GU* examination is the 48.___

    A. rectum   B. trachea   C. kidneys   D. pancreas

49. Of the following, the one which would be included in the x-ray examination known as a *GI* series is the 49.___

    A. colon   B. skull   C. lungs   D. uterus

50. A person who, while not ill himself, may transmit a disease to another person is known as a(n) 50.___

    A. breeder   B. incubator
    C. carrier   D. inhibitor

KEY (CORRECT ANSWERS)

1. D	11. B	21. B	31. B	41. D
2. C	12. A	22. C	32. B	42. C
3. A	13. B	23. A	33. A	43. D
4. A	14. D	24. B	34. B	44. A
5. D	15. A	25. D	35. D	45. C
6. C	16. C	26. D	36. A	46. B
7. B	17. A	27. C	37. A	47. B
8. A	18. D	28. C	38. B	48. C
9. C	19. C	29. A	39. C	49. A
10. C	20. A	30. D	40. A	50. C

TEST 2

DIRECTIONS: Each question or incomplete statement is followed by several suggested answers or completions. Select the one that BEST answers the question or completes the statement. *PRINT THE LETTER OF THE CORRECT ANSWER IN THE SPACE AT THE RIGHT.*

1. Thorough washing of the hands for two minutes with soap and warm water will leave the hands   1.____

    A. sterile   B. aseptic
    C. decontaminated   D. partially disinfected

2. The one of the following which is BEST for preparing the skin for an injection is   2.____

    A. green soap and water   B. alcohol
    C. phenol   D. formalin

3. A fever thermometer should be cleansed after use by washing it with   3.____

    A. soap and cool water   B. warm water only
    C. soap and hot water   D. running cold tap water

4. The FIRST step in cleaning an instrument which has fresh blood on it is to   4.____

    A. wash it in hot soapy water
    B. wash it under cool running water
    C. soak it in a boric acid bath
    D. soak it in 70% alcohol

5. If a contaminated nasal speculum cannot be sterilized immediately after use, then the BEST procedure to follow until sterilization is possible is to place it   5.____

    A. under a piece of dry gauze
    B. in warm water
    C. in alcohol
    D. in a green soap solution

6. A hypodermic needle should always be checked to see if it has a good sharp point   6.____

    A. when it is being washed
    B. when it is removed from the sterilizer
    C. just before it is sterilized
    D. immediately before an injection

7. Of the following, the LOWEST temperature at which cotton goods will be sterilized if placed in an autoclave for 30 minutes is _____°F.   7.____

    A. 130   B. 170   C. 200   D. 250

8. Of the following procedures, the one which is BEST for sterilizing an ear speculum which is contaminated with wax is to   8.____

A. scrub in with cold soapy water, rinse in ether, and place in boiling water for 20 minutes
B. soak it in warm water, scrub in cold soapy water, rinse with water, and autoclave at 275°F for 10 minutes
C. wash it in alcohol, scrub in hot soapy water, rinse with water, and place in boiling water for 20 minutes
D. wash it in 1% Lysol solution, rinse, and autoclave at 275°F for 15 minutes

9. Assume that clean water accidentally spilled on the outside of a package of cloth-wrapped hypodermic syringes which has been sterilized.
Of the following, the BEST action to take is to   9.__

A. leave the package to dry in a sunny, clean place
B. sterilize the package again
C. remove the wet cloth and wrap the package in a dry sterile cloth
D. wipe off the package with a clean dry towel and later ask the nurse in charge what to do

10. Hypodermic needles should be sterilized by placing them in   10.__

A. boiling water for 5 minutes
B. an autoclave at 15 lbs. pressure for 15 minutes
C. oil heated to 220°F for 10 minutes
D. a 1:40 Lysol solution for 10 minutes

11. A cutting instrument should be sterilized by placing it in   11.__

A. a chemical germicide
B. an autoclave at 15 lbs. pressure for 20 minutes
C. boiling water for 20 minutes
D. a hot air oven at 320°F for 1 hour

12. A fever thermometer used by a patient who has tuberculosis should be washed and then placed in _____ minute(s).   12.__

A. boiling water for 10
B. a hot air oven for 20
C. a 1:1000 solution of bichloride of mercury for one
D. an autoclave at 15 lbs. pressure for 15

13. The MOST reliable method of sterilizing a glass syringe is to place it in _____ minutes.   13.__

A. Zephiran chloride 1:1000 solution for 40
B. oil heated to 250°F for 12
C. boiling water for 20
D. an autoclave at 15 lbs. pressure for 20

14. The insides of sterilizers should be cleaned daily with a mild abrasive PRIMARILY to   14.__

A. remove scale
B. prevent the growth of bacteria
C. remove blood and other organic matter
D. prevent acids from damaging the sterilizer

15. Of the following, the BEST reason for giving a patient a jar in which to bring a urine spec-   15._____
    imen on his next visit to the clinic is that the

    A. patient may not have a jar at home
    B. patient may bring the specimen in a jar which is too large
    C. patient may bring the specimen in a jar which has not been cleaned properly
    D. jar may be misplaced if it is not a jar in which urine specimens are usually collected

16. Simply providing nutritional information and recommended low-cost diets to clinic   16._____
    patients has not resulted in improved diets for their children.
    The MOST plausible conclusion to draw from this statement is that

    A. nutrition is only one factor in improving health
    B. nutrition is of greater value in improving the health of adults than in improving the
       health of children
    C. the health problems of clinic patients are not caused by nutritional defects
    D. clinic patients are not using the nutritional information given them

17. Many people who appear to be robust are highly susceptible to disease, and are outlived   17._____
    by many seemingly frail people.
    Of the following, the MOST plausible conclusion which may be drawn from this state-
    ment is that

    A. physical appearance is not a reliable indicator of health
    B. frail people take better care of themselves than do robust people
    C. disease tends to strike robust people more frequently than frail people
    D. robust people tend to overexert themselves more often than frail people do

18. The skill of interviewers, the wording of questions, and the willingness of patients to   18._____
    respond freely to questions all affect the results of a survey. Reports of surveys of patient
    attitudes toward the health work of the clinic are, therefore, valueless unless we also
    know how the surveys were conducted. A recent report that 85% of clinic patients were
    satisfied with clinic service must be treated with caution; it may be that another survey
    would have revealed just the opposite!
    On the basis of this paragraph, it is MOST accurate to conclude that

    A. survey reports have little value in determining patient attitudes
    B. contrary to a recent report, 85% of clinic patients are dissatisfied with clinic service
    C. published results of surveys may be misleading unless accompanied by knowledge
       of the methods used
    D. listening to the unsolicited comments of clinic patients is of greater value than
       questioning them directly concerning their attitudes

Questions 19-25.

DIRECTIONS: Questions 19 through 25 are to be answered on the basis of the following table

STATISTICAL REPORT OF CLINICS IN XYZ HEALTH CENTER March				
	APPOINTMENTS		PROCEDURES	
Clinic	No. of Appointments Scheduled	No. of Broken Appointments	No. of Diagnostic Procedures	No. of Surgical Procedures
A	1400	260	1910	140
B	730	160	2000	500
C	1250	250	950	130
D	540	90	400	220
E	890	140	1500	280

19. On the basis of the preceding table, the total number of appointments kept for all clinics in the health center in March is   19.__

    A. 900   B. 3910   C. 4810   D. 5710

20. The percentage of appointments kept in Clinic C during March is   20.__

    A. 5%   B. 20%   C. 75%   D. 80%

21. If Clinic A was open for 20 days during March, the average number of appointments scheduled each day at Clinic A is   21.__

    A. 57   B. 70   C. 140   D. 280

22. In comparison to the clinic which performed the fewest diagnostic procedures, the clinic which performed the MOST diagnostic procedures did _____ as many.   22.__

    A. twice   B. three times
    C. four times   D. five times

23. The average number of diagnostic procedures performed for all clinics during March is   23.__

    A. 254   B. 676   C. 1352   D. 6760

24. The percentage of all procedures done at Clinic B during March which were surgical procedures is   24.__

    A. 2%   B. 2.5%   C. 20%   D. 25%

25. Clinic E used 10 boxes of gauze for its surgical procedures during March.
If Clinic A used gauze at the same rate for its surgical procedures, the number of boxes of gauze Clinic A used during March is   25.__

    A. 3   B. 5   C. 10   D. 14

Questions 26-34.

DIRECTIONS: Each of Questions 26 through 34 consists of four words. Three of these words belong together. One word does NOT belong with the other three. For each group of words, you are to select the one word which does NOT belong with the other three words.

26.   A. conclude   B. terminate   C. initiate   D. end   26.____

27.   A. deficient   B. inadequate   27.____
       C. excessive   D. insufficient

28.   A. rare   B. unique   C. unusual   D. frequent   28.____

29.   A. unquestionable   B. uncertain   29.____
       C. doubtful   D. indefinite

30.   A. stretch   B. contract   C. extend   D. expand   30.____

31.   A. accelerate   B. quicken   31.____
       C. accept   D. hasten

32.   A. sever   B. rupture   C. rectify   D. tear   32.____

33.   A. innocuous   B. injurious   C. dangerous   D. harmful   33.____

34.   A. adulterate   B. contaminate   34.____
       C. taint   D. disinfect

Questions 35-40.

DIRECTIONS: Questions 35 through 40 are to be answered on the basis of the usual rules for alphabetical filing. For each question, indicate in the space at the right the letter preceding the name which should be filed THIRD in alphabetical order.

35.   A. Russell Cohen   B. Henry Cohn   35.____
       C. Wesley Chambers   D. Arthur Connors

36.   A. Wanda Jenkins   B. Pauline Jennings   36.____
       C. Leslie Jantzenberg   D. Rudy Jensen

37.   A. Arnold Wilson   B. Carlton Willson   37.____
       C. Duncan Williamson   D. Ezra Wilston

38.   A. Joseph M. Buchman   B. Gustave Bozzerman   38.____
       C. Constantino Brunelli   D. Armando Buccino

39.   A. Barbara Waverly   B. Corinne Warterdam   39.____
       C. Dennis Waterman   D. Harold Wartman

40.   A. Jose Mejia   B. Bernard Mendelsohn   40.____
       C. Antonio Mejias   D. Richard Mazzitelli

Questions 41-50.

DIRECTIONS: Questions 41 through 50 are to be answered on the basis of the usual rules of filing. Column I lists, next to the numbers 91 to 100, the names of 10 clinic patients. Column II lists, next to the letters A to D, the headings of file drawers into which you are to place the records of these patients. For each question, indicate in the space at the right the letter preceding the heading of the file drawer in which the record should be filed.

COLUMN I	COLUMN II	
41. Frank Shea	A. Sab - Sej	41._
42. Rose Seaborn	B. Sek - Sio	42._
43. Samuel Smollin	C. Sip - Soo	43._
44. Thomas Shur	D. Sop - Syz	44._
45. Ben Schaefer		45._
46. Shirley Strauss		46._
47. Harry Spiro		47._
48. Dora Skelly		48._
49. Sylvia Smith		49._
50. Arnold Selz		50._

KEY (CORRECT ANSWERS)

1.	D	11.	A	21.	B	31.	C	41.	B
2.	B	12.	C	22.	D	32.	C	42.	A
3.	A	13.	D	23.	C	33.	A	43.	C
4.	B	14.	A	24.	C	34.	D	44.	B
5.	D	15.	C	25.	B	35.	B	45.	A
6.	C	16.	D	26.	C	36.	B	46.	D
7.	D	17.	A	27.	C	37.	A	47.	D
8.	C	18.	C	28.	D	38.	D	48.	C
9.	B	19.	B	29.	A	39.	C	49.	C
10.	B	20.	D	30.	B	40.	C	50.	B

EXAMINATION SECTION
TEST 1

DIRECTIONS: Each question or incomplete statement is followed by several suggested answers or completions. Select the one that BEST answers the question or completes the statement. *PRINT THE LETTER OF THE CORRECT ANSWER IN THE SPACE AT THE RIGHT.*

1. Penicillin is effective in the treatment of several diseases because it

    A. builds up bodily resistance to the disease
    B. builds an immunity to the organisms causing the disease
    C. halts the growth of disease-producing organisms
    D. kills the organisms which cause the disease

1.____

2. The HIGHEST incidence of tuberculosis occurs during the ages of

    A. 1-9   B. 10-14   C. 15-30   D. 31-45

2.____

3. The MOST infectious stage of measles is the

    A. febrile   B. convalescent   C. eruptive   D. coryzal

3.____

4. When caring for a child ill with measles, you should

    A. select a room which is light and airy, but should protect the child's eyes from direct light
    B. regulate the temperature of the room to about 72-75° F
    C. keep the child in a darkened room to protect its eyes
    D. have the child wear woolen clothing for warmth

4.____

5. Ringworm on the skin is caused by a

    A. bacterium   B. fungus   C. protozoan   D. worm

5.____

6. Body temperature taken by rectum is _____ body temperature taken orally.

    A. 1° lower than   B. the same as
    C. 1° higher than   D. 2° higher than

6.____

7. The dishes used by a patient ill with a communicable disease should be.

    A. scraped and rinsed, then washed
    B. soaked overnight in a strong disinfectant solution
    C. boiled for twenty minutes
    D. kept separate and washed with soap and hot water

7.____

8. Cold applications tend to

    A. decrease the supply of blood in the area to which they are applied
    B. dilate the blood vessels
    C. bring a greater supply of blood to the area to which they are applied
    D. increase the pressure on the nerve endings

8.____

9. A bed cradle is a useful device for 9.___

    A. elevating an extremity
    B. keeping the weight of the upper bed covers off the patient
    C. helping to keep a restless patient in bed
    D. allowing for the free circulation of air

10. If a patient shows signs of a pressure sore at the base of the spine, the nurse should 10.___

    A. try a sitting position for the patient
    B. use small cotton rings on the pressure spot
    C. apply an ointment to the sore
    D. place an air-ring under the patient's buttocks

11. If a patient lying on her side is uncomfortable, the nurse may give her a(n) 11.___

    A. extra top cover
    B. back rest
    C. snug abdominal bandage
    D. pillow to support the lumbar region

12. The diet for a patient with gallstones MAY include 12.___

    A. grapefruit juice   B. liver
    C. cream   D. peas

13. A rich source of vitamin K is 13.___

    A. butter   B. spinach   C. oranges   D. milk

14. Flaxseed meal is prescribed for making an application of moist heat because of its 14.___

    A. medicinal properties   B. mucilaginous ingredients
    C. lightness   D. ability to retain heat

15. Of the following, the substance that is NOT commonly used as an emetic is 15.___

    A. bicarbonate of soda   B. mustard powder
    C. syrup of ipecac   D. table salt

16. Supervised practice periods are USEFUL to 16.___

    A. insure continued practice on part of students
    B. prevent wrong bonds from becoming fixed through practice
    C. supplement class instruction
    D. teach children to study

17. The science of human behavior is called 17.___

    A. psychiatry   B. mental hygiene
    C. psychology   D. psychoanalysis

18. The microscopical examination of bacteria is used to determine 18.___

    A. best conditions for growth
    B. their virulency
    C. their size, shape, etc.
    D. their relation toward certain foods

19. A disease that confers active immunity is   19.____

    A. scarlet fever   B. erysipelas
    C. pneumonia   D. common colds

20. A SERIOUS infection of the eyes is   20.____

    A. trachoma   B. myopia
    C. astigmatism   D. amblyopia

21. A substance that inhibits the growth of bacteria but does NOT destroy them is called   21.____

    A. germicide   B. disinfectant
    C. antiseptic   D. sterilizer

22. Organisms which cause diseases of the intestinal tract are   22.____

    A. colon bacillus   B. diphtheria bacillus
    C. typhoid bacillus   D. cholera spirillum

23. Proved protection has been discovered against   23.____

    A. smallpox   B. mumps
    C. common colds   D. measles

24. Strabismus is COMMONLY known as   24.____

    A. near-sightedness   B. far-sightedness
    C. cross-eyes   D. pink eyes

25. The country that has the HIGHEST death rate of mothers in childbirth is   25.____

    A. England   B. Italy   C. China   D. United States

KEY (CORRECT ANSWERS)

1. C	11. D
2. C	12. A
3. D	13. B
4. A	14. D
5. B	15. A
6. C	16. C
7. C	17. C
8. A	18. C
9. B	19. A
10. D	20. A

21. B
22. C
23. A
24. C
25. C

———

TEST 2

DIRECTIONS: Each question or incomplete statement is followed by several suggested answers or completions. Select the one that BEST answers the question or completes the statement. *PRINT THE LETTER OF THE CORRECT ANSWER IN THE SPACE AT THE RIGHT.*

1. The one of the following which is NOT generally used to alleviate pain is   1.____

    A. aspirin   B. morphine   C. cocaine   D. quinine

2. The administration of a drug subcutaneously means administration by   2.____

    A. mouth
    B. injection beneath the skin
    C. application on the surface of the skin
    D. rectum

3. The one of the following which is NOT a disinfectant is   3.____

    A. boiling water   B. iodine
    C. formaldehyde   D. novocain

4. The one of the following which is LEAST related to the pulse rate of an individual is his   4.____

    A. blood pressure   B. temperature
    C. weight   D. emotional state

5. The one of the following which denotes normal vision is   5.____

    A. 20/10   B. 20/20   C. 20/30   D. 20/40

6. Of the following, the temperature which is MOST desirable for a babies' weighing room in a health center is   6.____

    A. 60-62° F   B. 65-68° F   C. 75-77° F   D. 85-88° F

7. Of the following, it is MOST advisable for the operator to wear dark glasses during treatments by   7.____

    A. x-ray   B. infra-red radiation
    C. diathermy   D. ultra-violet radiation

8. Of the following, the BEST method of sterilizing glassware for surgical purposes is by means of   8.____

    A. immersion in boiling water
    B. steaming under pressure
    C. cold sterilization
    D. washing thoroughly with soap and water

9. The apparatus used for sterilizing medical equipment by means of steam under pressure is the   9.____

    A. autoclave   B. manometer   C. catheter   D. reamer

10. After each use of a thermometer, it should be   10.___

    A. held under hot water for several minutes
    B. disinfected in a chemical solution
    C. rinsed in cold water
    D. wiped clean with cotton

11. The LEAST desirable action to take in administering first aid to a person suffering from   11.___
shock is to

    A. give the patient some aromatic spirits of ammonia
    B. place the patient in a reclining position and elevate his legs
    C. loosen any tight clothing and place a pillow under his head
    D. place a hot water bottle near the patient's feet

12. Of the following symptoms, the one which does NOT generally accompany a fainting   12.___
spell is

    A. a flushed face
    B. perspiration of the forehead
    C. shallow breathing
    D. a slow pulse

13. Assume that a six-year-old boy is brought to the clinic bleeding profusely from a scalp   13.___
wound. The doctor has not as yet arrived.
Of the following, the MOST effective action for you to take is to

    A. wash the wound thoroughly with soap and water to prevent infection, apply pressure on the bleeding point, then treat for shock
    B. place the boy in a comfortable position, apply tincture of iodine to the wound to prevent infection, then treat for shock
    C. give the patient a stimulant, then attempt to stop the bleeding by applying digital pressure
    D. make the boy comfortable, place a compress over the wound and bandage snugly, then treat for shock

14. Of the following, the MOST frequently used method for the diagnosis of pulmonary tuber-   14.___
culosis is the

    A. blood test   B. x-ray
    C. metabolism test   D. urinalysis

15. Of the following conditions, the one which MAY be infectious is   15.___

    A. diabetes   B. tuberculosis
    C. appendicitis   D. hypertension

16. Of the following, observation of deviations from normal body weight may aid LEAST in   16.___
determining the presence of

    A. glandular disturbances   B. malnutrition
    C. organic disturbances   D. mental deficiency

17. Leukemia is a disease of the blood characterized by a   17.____

    A. moderate increase in the red cell count and decrease in the white cell count
    B. marked decrease in the red cell count and an increase in the white cell count
    C. marked increase in the hemoglobin content
    D. marked decrease in the white cell count

18. The one of the following which is MOST commonly used in the treatment of arthritis is   18.____

    A. radium   B. an electrocardiogram
    C. a radiograph   D. diathermy

19. The fluoroscope is used CHIEFLY to   19.____

    A. provide a permanent picture of the condition of internal organs at a given time
    B. make a chart of the action of the muscles of the heart
    C. observe the internal structure and functioning of the organs of the body at a given time
    D. produce heat in the tissues of the body

20. A stethoscope is an instrument used for   20.____

    A. determining the blood pressure
    B. taking the body temperature
    C. chest examinations
    D. determining the amount of sugar in the blood

21. The Dick test is used to determine susceptibility to   21.____

    A. measles   B. scarlet fever
    C. diphtheria   D. chicken pox

22. The aorta is a(n)   22.____

    A. bone   B. artery   C. ligament   D. nerve

23. The esophagus is part of the   23.____

    A. alimentary canal   B. abdominal wall
    C. mucous membrane   D. circulatory system

24. Of the following, the one which is NOT a blood vessel is the   24.____

    A. vein   B. capillary   C. ganglion   D. artery

25. Vital statistics include data relating to   25.____

    A. births, deaths, and marriages
    B. the cost of food, clothing, and shelter
    C. the number of children per family unit
    D. diseases and their comparative mortality rates

KEY (CORRECT ANSWERS)

1.	D		11.	C
2.	B		12.	A
3.	D		13.	D
4.	C		14.	B
5.	B		15.	B
6.	C		16.	D
7.	D		17.	B
8.	B		18.	D
9.	A		19.	C
10.	B		20.	C

21.	B
22.	B
23.	A
24.	C
25.	A

————

TEST 3

DIRECTIONS: Each question or incomplete statement is followed by several suggested answers or completions. Select the one that BEST answers the question or completes the statement. *PRINT THE LETTER OF THE CORRECT ANSWER IN THE SPACE AT THE RIGHT.*

1. The food rich in vitamin A is
   1.____

   A. liver   B. butter   C. rice   D. soy beans

2. Vitamin B promotes
   2.____

   A. clear vision
   B. good digestion
   C. good dentition
   D. resistance to respiratory diseases

3. When very rapid action of a drug is desired, it is USUALLY given
   3.____

   A. in pill form   B. in a capsule
   C. by hot applications   D. hypodermic injection

4. Digestion takes place MOST extensively in the
   4.____

   A. mouth   B. large intestine
   C. stomach   D. small intestine

5. Faulty posture MOST frequently results from
   5.____

   A. a circulatory disorder   B. anemia
   C. foot defects   D. faulty nutrition

6. The chemical substances secreted by the endocrine glands are called
   6.____

   A. body builders   B. antibodies
   C. stimulants   D. hormones

7. The master or *key* gland in the body is known as the
   7.____

   A. thyroid   B. adrenal   C. thymus   D. pituitary

8. Hereditary susceptibility to disease means
   8.____

   A. having the germ of a disease within us at birth
   B. inheriting a disease which may later develop
   C. inheriting some physical characteristic which might be a determining factor in developing the disease
   D. congenital contraction of a specific disease

9. The DIRECT cause of local infection is
   9.____

   A. lowered resistance
   B. secondary anemia
   C. introduction of pathogenic organisms
   D. a break or tear in the skin

10. Sickroom visitors should be seated

    A. near the head of the bed out of sight of the patient but within hearing distance of the voice
    B. at the foot of the bed where the patient may see the visitor
    C. on a chair, at the side of the bed, within the patient's range of vision and hearing
    D. on a chair brought near enough to the bed so that the visitor may lean comfortably on the bed to see and hear the patient without difficulty

10.___

11. The incubation period is the

    A. time when the symptoms of illness appear
    B. period during which the disease-producing germ is developing in the body
    C. period during which the patient's excretions contain the disease-producing germs
    D. period when the patient is quarantined

11.___

12. The mouth care of a bed patient is

    A. given if the patient wants it
    B. given as part of the daily routine
    C. important only if the patient has a denture
    D. important only when the patient has fever

12.___

13. A device COMMONLY used to relieve pressure on the heels and elbows is

    A. an air cushion   B. gauze and cotton rings
    C. a bed cradle   D. a folded woolen blanket

13.___

14. The Schick test is given for determining susceptibility to

    A. scarlet fever   B. diphtheria
    C. smallpox   D. measles

14.___

15. A mustard footbath is USUALLY given to relieve

    A. convulsions
    B. nausea
    C. congestion in a distant area
    D. dizziness

15.___

16. The *mode of transmission* of a communicable disease is the

    A. medium by which the disease germ was carried to the patient
    B. point of attack
    C. source of the infectious agent
    D. incubation period

16.___

17. The foods that should be stressed in the diet for the prevention of constipation are:

    A. fruits, green vegetables, and whole grain cereals
    B. bran, and bran-filled cereals
    C. potatoes, meat, nuts, and white bread
    D. soups, bread, butter, and milk

17.___

18. Body temperature taken by rectum is   18.____

    A. 1° lower than oral   B. the same as oral
    C. 1° higher than oral   D. 2° higher than oral

19. The warm mustard footbath is prepared by   19.____

    A. mixing one cup of mustard and two quarts of water and boiling same
    B. soaking feet, rubbed with musterole, in hot water
    C. dissolving prepared mustard (one cup) in three quarts of hot water
    D. adding one tablespoon of mustard previously dissolved in cool water to four quarts of warm water

20. Medications given orally may be administered in the following form: 20.____

    A. Ampule   B. Injection   C. Inunction   D. Capsule

21. The dishes used by a patient ill with a communicable disease should be   21.____

    A. scraped and rinsed, then washed
    B. soaked overnight in a strong disinfectant solution
    C. boiled for twenty minutes
    D. kept separate and washed with soap and hot water

22. The temperature taken by mouth commonly accepted as normal is   22.____

    A. 99.6° F   B. 97.6° F   C. 98.6° F   D. 96.8° F

23. The nurse should administer medicine only when   23.____

    A. the patient feels ill
    B. recommended as safe by a licensed druggist
    C. ordered by the physician
    D. the symptoms indicate the need of medication

24. The MOST important duty of the nurse is to   24.____

    A. do everything herself
    B. protect the patient from visitors
    C. have full charge of carrying out orders and nursing procedures
    D. constantly reassure the patient

25. An infectious agent is   25.____

    A. a disease
    B. the organism that causes a disease
    C. the place where the germ is found
    D. the person who carries the disease

KEY (CORRECT ANSWERS)

1. B	11. B
2. B	12. B
3. D	13. B
4. D	14. B
5. D	15. C
6. D	16. A
7. D	17. A
8. C	18. C
9. C	19. D
10. C	20. D

21. C
22. C
23. C
24. C
25. B

———

TEST 4

DIRECTIONS: Each question or incomplete statement is followed by several suggested answers or completions. Select the one that BEST answers the question or completes the statement. *PRINT THE LETTER OF THE CORRECT ANSWER IN THE SPACE AT THE RIGHT.*

1. Vitamin A helps to prevent   1.____

   A. night blindness   B. beri-beri
   C. sterility   D. hemorrhage

2. When a simple enema has been ordered for the patient, the enema bag or can should be   2.____

   A. three feet above the level of the mattress
   B. six feet above the level of the mattress
   C. at a level to cause a moderate flow
   D. even with the head of the bed

3. Of the methods listed, the MOST satisfactory one for preventing the spread of the com-   3.____
   mon cold is

   A. administering antitoxin
   B. administering sulpha drugs
   C. isolation of the patient
   D. avoiding crowded places

4. The germ theory of disease was formulated by   4.____

   A. Harvey   B. Roentgen   C. Pasteur   D. Trudeau

5. The stomach is located in the _____ region.   5.____

   A. epigastric   B. hypogastric
   C. right lumbar   D. umbilical

6. Good dentition is BEST promoted by   6.____

   A. adequate diet
   B. brushing the teeth after eating
   C. routine visits to the dentist
   D. a quart of milk daily

7. Bacteria thrive BEST under conditions of   7.____

   A. light, moisture, and cold
   B. sunlight, moisture, and heat
   C. heat, moisture, and a food medium
   D. darkness, cold, and dryness

8. The test to measure food energy in the body is called _____ test.   8.____

   A. mechanical ingestion   B. chemical ingestion
   C. basal metabolism   D. endocrine balance

9. The hot water bottle is a GOOD medium for the application of 9.__

    A. dry heat   B. moist heat
    C. a counter-irritant   D. hydro-therapy

10. Cold applications tend to 10.__

    A. decrease the supply of blood in the area to which they are applied
    B. dilate the blood vessels
    C. bring a greater supply of blood to the area to which they are applied
    D. increase the pressure on the nerve endings

11. An acute ear infection is MOST often caused by 11.__

    A. a respiratory disease   B. sitting in a draft
    C. poor nutrition   D. lack of sleep

12. Red blood corpuscles which form the residue, after the serum has been removed for processing, are called 12.__

    A. gamma globulin   B. antigen
    C. antitoxin   D. plasma

13. Insulin shock therapy is COMMONLY used in the treatment of 13.__

    A. dementia praecox   B. malaria
    C. neuroses   D. diabetes

14. The test given to determine the individual's susceptibility to scarlet fever is the _____ test. 14.__

    A. Dick   B. Schick   C. Mantoux   D. Widal

15. Diabetes is a deficiency disease caused by the lack of an internal secretion manufactured in the 15.__

    A. adrenal cortex   B. islands of Langerhans
    C. pineal gland   D. ductless glands

16. Tuberculosis is classifed as a disease which is 16.__

    A. inherited   B. environmental
    C. caused by diet deficiency   D. non-communicable

17. The mineral known to be an important factor in the coagulation power of blood and the control of muscle contraction is 17.__

    A. iodine   B. calcium   C. phosphorus   D. iron

18. A carrier is a 18.__

    A. fly or other insect which may carry a disease-producing germ
    B. person who harbors the disease germs within his body but does not show symptoms of the disease
    C. person not immune to a disease
    D. disease-producing germ which may be carried from one person to another by some insect

19. A famous Belgian physician who wrote a book on human anatomy was   19.____

    A. Ehrlich   B. Lister   C. Domagk   D. Vesalius

20. Hemerolopia is   20.____

    A. night blindness   B. day blindness
    C. intestinal bleeding   D. dysmenorrhea

21. A bed cradle is a USEFUL device for   21.____

    A. elevating an extremity
    B. keeping the weight of the upper bed covers off the patient
    C. helping to keep a restless patient in bed
    D. allowing for the free circulation of air

22. At the termination of a communicable disease, the patient's room should be   22.____

    A. fumigated with sulphur
    B. disinfected with lysol
    C. allowed to remain unoccupied for 48 hours
    D. scrubbed thoroughly with soap and hot water and aired

23. Three ESSENTIALS of good ventilation are   23.____

    A. no drafts, humidity low, temperature high
    B. sufficient moisture, warmth, and fresh air
    C. humidity high, temperature low, air cool
    D. air in motion, correct temperature, and humidity

24. In order to guide the mental growth and normal development of the pre-school child, we should   24.____

    A. take advantage of his readiness to learn in a secure environment
    B. tell him exactly *what* to do and *how* to do the task
    C. guide him each step of the way
    D. correct him and reward him frequently

25. The technical term for vitamin B1 is   25.____

    A. nicotinic acid   B. thiamine chloride
    C. ascorbic acid   D. niacin

KEY (CORRECT ANSWERS)

1.	A		11.	A
2.	C		12.	A
3.	C		13.	A
4.	C		14.	A
5.	A		15.	B
6.	A		16.	B
7.	C		17.	B
8.	C		18.	B
9.	A		19.	D
10.	A		20.	B

21.	B
22.	D
23.	D
24.	A
25.	B

————

EXAMINATION SECTION
TEST 1

DIRECTIONS: Each question or incomplete statement is followed by several suggested answers or completions. Select the one that BEST answers the question or completes the statement. *PRINT THE LETTER OF THE CORRECT ANSWER IN THE SPACE AT THE RIGHT.*

1. A sponge rubber mattress will help to prevent pressure sores because it exerts   1.___
   - A. pressure only on the extremities
   - B. no pressure on the heavier parts of the body
   - C. no pressure on the body
   - D. equal pressure on all parts of the body

2. A physiological change in vision common in old age results in   2.___
   - A. farsightedness
   - B. nearsightedness
   - C. double vision
   - D. lack of coordination

3. Active immunity can be induced artificially by injecting a specific   3.___
   - A. antibody
   - B. antigen
   - C. immune serum
   - D. gamma globulin

4. During very warm or hot weather, the physiological effect often observed is   4.___
   - A. *decreased* blood supply to the skin
   - B. *decreased* urinary output
   - C. *increased* muscle tone
   - D. *increased* heat loss by radiation

5. The purpose of soap in an enema is to   5.___
   - A. promote temporary retention of water
   - B. destroy organisms in the colon
   - C. increase the surface tension of water
   - D. irritate the mucous membrane

6. Normally, blood pressure is the LOWEST in the   6.___
   - A. arteries
   - B. capillaries
   - C. veins
   - D. small arteries

7. Usually the FIRST permanent tooth to erupt is the   7.___
   - A. first molar
   - B. upper central incisor
   - C. lower central incisor
   - D. first premolar

8. A mercury clinical thermometer is the MOST accurate of all thermometers because mercury has a   8.___
   - A. low boiling point
   - B. change in physical state at body temperature
   - C. relatively uniform rate of expansion
   - D. moderate rate of heat conduction

9. The INCORRECTLY matched procedure and purpose is
    A. catheterization - obtaining a specimen of urine
    B. cold compresses - delaying suppurative processes
    C. hypodermoclysis - giving fluids
    D. gastric gavage - washing out the stomach

10. Increasing the angle between two bones is termed
    A. flexion   B. extension
    C. abduction   D. adduction

9.

10.

_____

KEY (CORRECT ANSWERS)

1. D	6. C
2. A	7. A
3. B	8. C
4. B	9. D
5. D	10. B

_____

TEST 2

DIRECTIONS: Each question or incomplete statement is followed by several suggested answers or completions. Select the one that BEST answers the question or completes the statement. *PRINT THE LETTER OF THE CORRECT ANSWER IN THE SPACE AT THE RIGHT.*

1. A method of control for communicable diseases that has been largely discarded is
   A. isolation of the patient
   B. immunization of children
   C. exclusion of contacts from school
   D. regulations governing garbage disposal

   1.___

2. Salt is restricted in a cardiac diet because salt will
   A. promote retention of fluid in the tissues
   B. decrease the permeability of the blood cell membrane
   C. impair the elasticity of the blood vessels
   D. cling to the lining of the blood vessels

   2.___

3. A piece of food remains lodged in the throat of a child. The immediate action MOST advisable is to
   A. dislodge the food with your finger
   B. dislodge the food with cotton
   C. hold the child upside down and slap its back
   D. give artificial respiration

   3.___

4. The emergency treatment to be employed FIRST when any chemical gets into the eye is to
   A. wash the eye out with large quantities of water
   B. put several drops of clean olive oil into the eye
   C. cover the eye with a sterile compress and call a doctor
   D. find out the antidote and administer it

   4.___

5. Salts may exert a diuretic effect because they are
   A. excreted as solutes
   B. irritating to the urinary bladder
   C. absorbed rapidly
   D. dehydrating

   5.___

6. The MOST important factor in selecting a chemical disinfectant is
   A. the type of microorganism to be killed
   B. its toxic effect on the tissue
   C. the simplicity of the method to be used
   D. the length of time required for disinfection

   6.___

7. An articulation of the body where MOST types of movements can be demonstrated is the
   A. ankle   B. knee   C. shoulder   D. wrist

   7.___

8. The mechanical body act which is NOT a natural defense mechanism against infectious agents is the
   A. tearing of the eyes
   B. churning of food in the stomach
   C. filtering of blood by the lymph glands
   D. coughing reflex

9. In the administration of oxygen, moisture is added to the oxygen to reduce the
   A. fire hazard
   B. water evaporation from mucous membranes
   C. surface tension
   D. kindling temperature

10. The CORRECT body alignment for a patient lying on the side is with the
    A. head in a straight line with the spine and knees slightly flexed
    B. shoulders rotated slightly forward and head tipped forward
    C. torso in a straight line and legs extended
    D. shoulders straight, legs extended, and head tipped slightly backward

____

KEY (CORRECT ANSWERS)

1.	C	6.	A
2.	A	7.	C
3.	C	8.	B
4.	A	9.	B
5.	A	10.	A

____

TEST 3

DIRECTIONS: Each question or incomplete statement is followed by several suggested answers or completions. Select the one that BEST answers the question or completes the statement. *PRINT THE LETTER OF THE CORRECT ANSWER IN THE SPACE AT THE RIGHT.*

1. Penicillin is effective in the treatment of several
   diseases because it
   A. builds up bodily resistance to the disease
   B. builds an immunity to the organisms causing the disease
   C. halts the growth of disease-producing organisms
   D. kills the organisms which cause the disease

   1.___

2. The HIGHEST incidence of tuberculosis occurs during the
   ages of
   A. 1-9   B. 10-14   C. 15-30   D. 31-45

   2.___

3. The MOST infectious stage of measles is the
   A. febrile   B. convalescent
   C. eruptive   D. coryzal

   3.___

4. The nurse, when caring for a child ill with measles,
   should
   A. select a room which is light and airy, but should
      protect the child's eyes from direct light
   B. regulate the temperature of the room to about 72-75°F
   C. keep the child in a darkened room to protect its eyes
   D. have the child wear woolen clothing for warmth

   4.___

5. Ringworm on the skin is caused by a
   A. bacterium B. fungus   C. protozoan   D. worm

   5.___

6. Body temperature taken by rectum is _____ body temperature
   taken orally.
   A. 1° lower than   B. the same as
   C. 1° higher than   D. 2° higher than

   6.___

7. The dishes used by a patient ill with a communicable
   disease should be
   A. scraped and rinsed, then washed
   B. soaked overnight in a strong disinfectant solution
   C. boiled for twenty minutes
   D. kept separate and washed with soap and hot water

   7.___

8. Cold applications tend to
   A. decrease the supply of blood in the area to which
      they are applied
   B. dilate the blood vessels
   C. bring a greater supply of blood to the area to which
      they are applied
   D. increase the pressure on the nerve endings

   8.___

9. A bed cradle is a useful device for
   A. elevating an extremity
   B. keeping the weight of the upper bed covers off the patient
   C. helping to keep a restless patient in bed
   D. allowing for the free circulation of air

10. If a patient shows signs of a pressure sore at the base of the spine, the home nurse should
   A. try a sitting position for the patient
   B. use small cotton wings on the pressure spot
   C. apply an ointment to the sore
   D. place an air-ring under the patient's buttocks

KEY (CORRECT ANSWERS)

1. C		6. C
2. C		7. C
3. D		8. A
4. A		9. B
5. B		10. D

TEST 4

DIRECTIONS: Each question or incomplete statement is followed by several suggested answers or completions. Select the one that BEST answers the question or completes the statement. *PRINT THE LETTER OF THE CORRECT ANSWER IN THE SPACE AT THE RIGHT.*

1. A NORMAL postural characteristic of a child learning to stand and walk is
   A. inverted toes
   B. kyphosis
   C. lordosis
   D. scoliosis

   1.___

2. The return of venous blood to the heart is NOT dependent upon
   A. contractions of the skeletal muscles
   B. breathing
   C. relaxation of the atria
   D. extensibility of the venous wall

   2.___

3. Cyanosis in a child *holding his breath* during a violent crying spell is due to a lack of oxygen in the blood as a result of a
   A. prolonged inspiration
   B. prolonged expiration
   C. venous blood supply to the face
   D. lack of arterial blood supply to face

   3.___

4. The purpose of a plaster cast is to
   A. produce traction
   B. reduce the fracture
   C. immobilize the bone
   D. straighten the bone

   4.___

5. In lifting a patient from a low plane, the nurse should NOT
   A. lower her own center of gravity
   B. flex her own knees
   C. exert the patient's weight against her vertebral axis
   D. keep her own feet together

   5.___

6. If a patient lying on her side is uncomfortable, the nurse may give her a(n)
   A. extra top cover
   B. snug abdominal bandage
   C. back rest
   D. pillow to support the lumbar region

   6.___

7. The diet for a patient with gallstones may include
   A. grapefruit juice
   B. liver
   C. cream
   D. peas

   7.___

8. A rich source of vitamin K is   8.
    A. butter   B. spinach   C. oranges   D. milk

9. Flaxseed meal is prescribed for making an application of   9.
moist heat because of its
    A. medicinal properties   B. mucilaginous ingredients
    C. lightness   D. ability to retain heat

10. Of the following, the substance that is NOT commonly used   10.
as an emetic is
    A. bicarbonate of soda   B. mustard powder
    C. syrup of ipecac   D. table salt

———

KEY (CORRECT ANSWERS)

1. C		6. D	
2. D		7. A	
3. B		8. B	
4. C		9. D	
5. D		10. A	

———

EXAMINATION SECTION

TEST 1

DIRECTIONS

Each question or incomplete statement is followed by several suggested answers or completions. Select the one that *BEST* answers the question or completes the statement. *PRINT THE LETTER OF THE CORRECT ANSWER IN THE SPACE AT THE RIGHT.*

1. If the label on the bottle of sodium bicarbonate reads   1. ...
   "0.32 gm. in 4cc," when the dosage ordered is grs, XV,
   you *should* give
      A. 0.15 gm   B. 0.20 gm   C. 0.44 gm   D. 0.96 gm
2. In preparing to administer morphine, sulfate gr 1/8 (h)   2. ...
   from tablets 0.010 gm, the accurate dosage *would be*
      A. 1/3 tablet   B. 1/2 tablet
      C. 3/4 tablet   D. 4/5 tablet
3. If the label reads "Acetylsalicylic Acid 0.32 gm (grams)"   3. ...
   for a 10-grain dosage, you *should* give
      A. 2 tablets B. 4 tablets C. 5 tablets D. 8 tablets
4. According to Young's Rule, a child of 8 years will receive 4. ...
      A. $\frac{2}{5}$ of the adult dosage   B. $\frac{1}{3}$ of the adult dosage

      C. $\frac{1}{2}$ of the adult dosage   D. $\frac{4}{5}$ of the adult dosage
5. The dietary treatment of diabetes mellitus includes: 5. ...
      A. Equalizing intake of proteins, carbohydrates, and fats
      B. Giving carbohydrates with restriction and adjusting
         intake of insulin
      C. Rigid restriction of carbohydrates and increased in-
         take of fats
      D. Maintenance of body weight at optimal level
6. In cardiac disease, the purpose of the low sodium diet   6. ...
   is to
      A. relieve edema
      B. increase kidney function by changing the salt balance
      C. reduce weight through decrease of appetite
      D. make sure that the patient is salt free
7. In fat-controlled diets,   7. ...
      A. all fats are restricted
      B. fatty meats are restricted; dairy foods are unrestricted
      C. poly-unsaturated fats are substituted for saturated fats
      D. roast chicken is the preferred protein
8. Of the following, the procedure which *violates* a law of   8. ...
   physics and increases fatigue is:
      A. Working with the patient in center of bed
      B. Carrying a basin of water close to body
      C. Carrying a basin by placing palms flat around the sides
      D. Standing with feet apart
9. The explanation of the fact that the comfort of the   9. ...
   patient is related to the height of the headrest is: The
      A. *higher* the headrest, the *greater* the distribution of
         body weight

    B. *lower* the headrest, the *greater* the distribution of
       body weight

    C. *lower* the headrest, the *greater* the strain on the
       sacrum

    D. *lower* the headrest, the *greater* the pressure on the
       buttocks

10. The "storage battery" which releases muscular energy   10. ...
instantly when a nerve impulse gives the order is a
complex phosphate molecule commonly known as
    A. FAO   B. ATP   C. WHO   D. ITO

11. It is dangerous for a patient with a suspected malignancy 11. ...
of the gastro-intestinal tract to take sodium bicarbonate
over an extended period of time because
    A. it hastens calcium metastasis
    B. its acidity is injurious to the tract lining
    C. it interferes with secretion of bile
    D. temporary relief pacifies the patient

12. The *approved* water temperature for the hot water bottle   12. ...
is:
    A. 105 degrees F - 115 degrees F
    B. 115 degrees F - 130 degrees F
    C. 120 degrees F - 150 degrees F
    D. 130 degrees F - 150 degrees F

13. Of the following items, the *one* that does *NOT* belong in   13. ...
the home medicine cabinet is
    A. an antiseptic   B. a lubricant
    C. a laxative   D. first-aid supplies

14. The value of the round-the-clock "q-4-h" temperature has   14. ...
been questioned because
    A. temperature has become less important in the treatment
       of disease
    B. it is known to vary with the time of day, month, age
    C. it is known to vary with individuals
    D. it wastes time of nursing personnel

15. Decubitus ulcers in bed-ridden patients are *BEST* avoided   15. ...
by the use of
    A. plasticized rings
    B. rubberized terry cotton draw sheets
    C. sheepskin   D. polyurethane foam

16. The deciduous set of teeth does *NOT* contain   16. ...
    A. cuspids B. lateral incisors C. bicuspids D. canines

17. Adequate thermometer care is   17. ...
    A. soap, water, friction   B. aqueous zephiran
    C. isoprophl alcohol 70%   D. alcohol 70%

18. The assimilation of calcium and phosphorus in the body   18. ...
depends upon the intake of vitamin
    A. A   B. C   C. D   D. E

19. Gamma globulin is a protein blood fraction that carries   19. ...
antibodies. When injected, it provides
    A. acquired immunity   B. active immunity
    C. passive immunity   D. artificial immunity

20. On the centigrade scale, the reading of normal mouth   20. ...
temperature, 98.6° F, is
    A. 32° C   B. 37° C   C. 37.6° C   D. 40° C

21. The oral (Sabin) vaccine against poliomyelitis contains   21. ...
    A. inactivated polioviruses B. live attenuated polioviruses
    C. specific polio antibodies
    E. live monkey serum
22. Nursing care of the sick at home should be planned   22. ...
    around the
    A. needs of the patient   B. household routines
    C. economic status of the family
    D. needs of the family
23. Of the following, the vitamin that is *NOT* fat-soluble   23. ...
    is
    A. A   B. B   C. E   D. K
24. The *SLOWEST* of all sense organs to develop is   24. ...
    A. taste   B. smell   C. sight   D. hearing
25. The reaction upon which the tuberculin test is based is   25. ...
    A. agglutination   B. allergy
    C. antibody production   D. precipitation

———

KEY (CORRECT ANSWERS)

1. D		11. D
2. D		12. B
3. C		13. C
4. A		14. A
5. D		15. D
6. A		16. C
7. C		17. A
8. A		18. C
9. B		19. C
10. B		20. B

21. B
22. A
23. B
24. C
25. B

———

TEST 2

DIRECTIONS:

Each question or incomplete statement is followed by several suggested answers or completions. Select the one that *BEST* answers the question or completes the statement. *PRINT THE LETTER OF THE CORRECT ANSWER IN THE SPACE AT THE RIGHT.*

1. Radioactive carbon is a tracer element used to study the   1. ...
     A. manufacture of erythrocytes
     B. motor nerve responses to stimuli
     C. path of certain food elements
     D. activity of certain endocrine glands

2. Mephenesin is used as a   2. ...
     A. tranquillizer   B. respiratory stimulant
     C. muscle relaxant   D. respiratory depressant

3. Dextrostix are used as a one-minute test for sugar in the   3. ...
     A. urine   B. spinal fluid
     C. gastric juice   D. blood

4. Cleft palate and hare lip have been developed in animals   4. ...
     by depriving prospective animal mothers of certain
     vitamins during the period when the foetus' jaw and
     mouth are being formed. These vitamins are certain B
     vitamins *and* vitamin
     A. A   B. C   C. D   D. E

5. Edathamil calcium disodium may be administered before   5. ...
     brain damage occurs in cases of diagnosed
     A. phenylketonuria   B. Wilson's disease
     C. lead poisoning   D. secondary anemia

6. Eggs contain an emulsifier of cholesterol known as   6. ...
     A. lysine   B. lecithen   C. acetylcholine   D. trypsin

7. To ease the chronic shortage of high quality human bone   7. ...
     available from bone bands, the Federal Drug Administra-
     tion has approved the detailed processing of
     A. yearling lamb bones   B. six-months-old lamb bones
     C. six-weeks-old calves' bones
     D. two-years-old cows' bones

8. The one-shot so-called "health gift" of measles vaccine   8. ...
     contains
     A. dead measles virus   B. live measles virus
     C. mixed dead virus   D. mixed live virus

9. The diet prescribed for a phenylketonuria which may pre-   9. ...
     vent brain damage is one that is
     A. *low* in fruits and vegetables, *high* in protein
     B. *high* in fruits, vegetables, and animal protein
     C. a commercially available protein substitute
     D. vegetables, fruits, and a commercially available
        protein substitute

10. The Haversian Canals are associated with the   10. ...
     A. secretion of anterior pituitary gland
     B. aqueous humor in the eye
     C. excretion of pancreatic juice
     D. structure of long bones

11. A colles fracture is associated with the fracture of   11. ...
     A. the lower third of the tibia - fibula

4

B. the lower third of the radius
C. a lumbar vertebra   D. the upper third of the femus

12. In muscles undergoing contraction, irritability and   12. ...
fatigue may result from an accumulation of
    A. phosphoric acid   B. carbon dioxide and lactic acid
    C. glycogen   D. creatine

13. In the care of a patient who has suffered a cerebral   13. ...
vascular accident, the nurse's *FIRST* concern is
    A. rehabilitation of the patient
    B. helping to restore the confidence of the patient
    C. survival of the patient   D. careful feeding

14. The procedure *MOST* frequently used to withdraw a small   14. ...
amount of spinal fluid for diagnosis is called a
    A. lumbar puncture   B. cisternal puncture
    C. pneumoencephalogram   D. ventriculogram

15. An infection of the kidney pelvis and the spread of the   15. ...
infection to the kidney tissue results in a condition
known as
    A. hydronephrosis   B. nephrosclerosis
    C. nephritis   D. pyelonephritis

16. An *alternate* for insulin therapy in some cases of   16. ...
diabetes is therapy using
    A. sulfadiazine   B. sulfaguanidine
    C. sulfapyrimidine   D. sulfonylurea

17. When there is severe bleeding, it is usually *best* to   17. ...
IMMEDIATELY
    A. apply a sterile dressing   B. apply a tourniquet
    C. apply a pressure bandage   D. elevate the area

18. The *PRIMARY* function of protein in the body is to   18. ...
    A. supply material for growth and repair of body tissues
    B. supply energy
    C. aid in the proper utilization of other nutrients
    D. transport vitamins and minerals to various parts of
       the body

19. *Good* diagnostic procedures used to give information   19. ...
about the heart are:
    A. Chest x-ray and electro-cardiogram
    B. Fluoroscopy and cardiac catheterization
    C. Lipiodal x-ray and B.M.R.
    D. Complete blood count and urinalysis

20. To avoid gastric irritation by frequent large doses of   20. ...
acetylsalicylic acid, the physician orders
    A. buffered tablets   B. salicylic acid tablets
    C. aluminum hydroxide gel   D. enteric coated tablets

21. The respiratory center is located in the   21. ...
    A. medulla oblongata   B
    B. occipital lobe of the cerebrum
    C. corpus callosum   D. cerebellum

22. The anatomical structure which performs the function of   22. ...
the nervous system is the
    A. neuroglia   B. fibers of Remak
    C. neuron   D. exteroceptors

23. Disruption of the erythrocyte membrane which leads to the   23. ...
cells' hemoglobin content going into solution in the
plasma is known as

5

A. agglutination
B. phagocytosis
C. hemolysis
D. hemopoiesis

24. The *cause* of primary anemia is   24. ...
   A. the inability of the patient to produce the erythrocyte maturation factor
   B. a poor nutritional pattern causing lack of hemoglobin
   C. sudden loss of large amounts of blood
   D. hereditary and may appear in any generation

25. Extensive superficial frostbite should be treated as   25. ...
deep frostbite, using a bacteriostatic agent and whirl-pool bath of _____ water.
   A. cool   B. warm   C. hot   D. cold

KEY (CORRECT ANSWERS)

#	Ans		#	Ans
1.	C		11.	B
2.	D		12.	B
3.	A		13.	C
4.	A		14.	A
5.	C		15.	D
6.	B		16.	D
7.	C		17.	C
8.	B		18.	A
9.	D		19.	B
10.	D		20.	D

21. A
22. C
23. C
24. A
25. B

EXAMINATION SECTION
TEST 1

DIRECTIONS: Each question or incomplete statement is followed by several suggested answers or completions. Select the one that BEST answers the question or completes the statement. *PRINT THE LETTER OF THE CORRECT ANSWER IN THE SPACE AT THE RIGHT.*

1. A nurse instructing a family in the home should emphasize that of the following the MOST effective way of controlling tuberculosis infection is to   1.____

    A. soak all the patient's linen in soap and water solution for 6 hours before laundering
    B. admit no one to the room except the attendant
    C. have the patient cover his mouth and nose with disposable tissues when coughing or expectorating
    D. remove all rugs, curtains, and unnecessary furniture from the room

2. When a post-operative patient complains of pain in the calf of the leg, aggravated by dorsiflexion of the foot, the BEST course of action for the nurse to take is to recommend   2.____

    A. hot soakings
    B. walking about to relieve pain
    C. massaging locally
    D. remaining in bed and calling the doctor

3. Morbidity rates are statistics relative to   3.____

    A. births
    C. sickness and disease
    B. deaths
    D. marriages

4. The Snellen test is a   4.____

    A. visual screening test
    C. blood test for anemia
    B. diagnostic test for syphilis
    D. hearing test

5. The nurse should instruct families that the temperature of water for hot water bottles should be between   5.____

    A. 95° and 110° F
    C. 135° and 150° F
    B. 115° and 130° F
    D. 155° and 170° F

6. When planning a feeding schedule for a premature infant, it is of PRIMARY importance to   6.____

    A. feed the baby regularly every two hours
    B. establish a food tolerance since the intestinal tract is undeveloped
    C. include Vitamins A, B, C, D and K in the feeding
    D. provide for additional carbohydrates

7. B.C.G. vaccine is being given at the present time   7.____

    A. to all children with a positive tuberculin test
    B. to all children exposed to tuberculosis

    C.   to all children with minimal tuberculosis lesions
    D.   experimentally to non-reactors to the tuberculin test who are subject to frequent exposure to tuberculosis

8.   When teaching a colostomy patient self-care at home, the MOST important point for the nurse to emphasize is that   8.

    A.   a colostomy bag is essential to assure safety from leakage
    B.   the irrigation can should hang five feet above hip level
    C.   the irrigation should be done at the same time each day
    D.   the irrigation should be followed by one hour of bed-rest

9.   The destruction of all organisms, including spores, is known as   9.

    A.   disinfection   B.   sterilization
    C.   antiseptic action   D.   germicidal action

10.   The MOST frequent and serious complication likely to arise after a patient has undergone surgery is   10.

    A.   wound infection   B.   blood poisoning
    C.   respiratory infection   D.   decubitus ulcers

11.   A disarrangement of the normal relation of the bones entering into the formation of a joint BEST defines   11.

    A.   a dislocation   B.   a fracture
    C.   a sprain   D.   ankylosis

12.   The Non-Protein Nitrogen (N.P.N.) test is a   12.

    A.   blood test to determine renal function
    B.   blood test to determine liver function
    C.   urine test to determine concentration
    D.   patency test of the Fallopian tubes

13.   When eating pork, a person may AVOID trichinosis by   13.

    A.   not eating it in warm weather
    B.   soaking it in salt water two hours before cooking
    C.   buying pork which has a government inspection stamp
    D.   thoroughly cooking it

14.   Beriberi is a nutritional disease caused by lack of a sufficient amount of vitamin   14.

    A. A   B. B_1 C. B_{12} D. K

15.   The one of the following groups of foods which is the BEST source of thiamine is   15.

    A.   milk, egg yolks, cheese, lettuce
    B.   green peas, broccoli, kale, cabbage
    C.   escarole, carrots, cream cheese
    D.   whole grain bread and cereals, pork, organ meats

16. The vitamin believed to be of GREATEST aid in the healing of wounds is vitamin   16._____

    A. B_2 B. B_{12} C. C   D. D

17. Following the ingestion of contaminated food, acute food poisoning USUALLY occurs   17._____
after the elapse of from _____ hours.

    A. 2 to 6   B. 7 to 12
    C. 13 to 24   D. 25 to 36

18. A slowly progressive degenerative disease of the nervous system usually occurring in or   18._____
after middle life, and characterized by tremors and rigidity of the skeletal muscles, BEST
defines the condition known as

    A. arthritis   B. Parkinson's disease
    C. Jacksonian epilepsy   D. multiple sclerosis

19. Of the following, the PREFERRED site for intramuscular injections is   19._____

    A. the deltoid muscle
    B. the quadriceps muscle
    C. any section of the buttocks
    D. the upper outer quadrant of the buttock near its inner angle

20. Of the following, the one which is MALIGNANT is   20._____

    A. papilloma   B. lipoma
    C. lymphosarcoma   D. myoma

21. Of the following organisms, the one which causes MORE THAN HALF of all kidney infec-   21._____
tions is

    A. bacterium coli   B. staphylocoecus
    C. streptococcus   D. escherichia coli

22. Of the following antibiotics, the one which produces a TOXIC effect on the auditory nerve   22._____
is

    A. chloromycetin   B. aureomycin
    C. streptomycin   D. penicillin

23. Antibiotics are UNIFORMLY excreted through the   23._____

    A. skin   B. urine   C. stool   D. lungs

24. Isonicotinic acid hydrazide is used CHIEFLY in the treatment of   24._____

    A. rheumatic fever   B. arthritis
    C. cancer   D. tuberculosis

25. The one of the following which attacks the enamel of the teeth is   25._____

    A. gingivitis   B. dental caries
    C. pyorrhea alveolaris   D. vitamin C deficiency

KEY (CORRECT ANSWERS)

1.	C	11.	A
2.	D	12.	A
3.	C	13.	D
4.	A	14.	B
5.	B	15.	D
6.	B	16.	C
7.	D	17.	B
8.	C	18.	B
9.	D	19.	D
10.	C	20.	C

21.	A
22.	C
23.	B
24.	D
25.	B

TEST 2

DIRECTIONS: Each question or incomplete statement is followed by several suggested answers or completions. Select the one that BEST answers the question or completes the statement. *PRINT THE LETTER OF THE CORRECT ANSWER IN THE SPACE AT THE RIGHT.*

1. Failure of muscle coordination to bring the image of an object upon the fovea centralis retinae at the same time in each eye BEST defines the condition known as

    A. glaucoma
    C. retrobulbar neuritis
    B. optic neuritis
    D. strabismus

1.____

2. ANOTHER term for farsightedness is

    A. hyperopia
    C. ophthalmia
    B. myopia
    D. astigmatism

2.____

3. A condition which in its advanced stages is characterized by symptoms of halos or rainbows around light is known as

    A. cataracts
    C. glaucoma
    B. detached retina
    D. corneal ulcers

3.____

4. Blocking of the eustachian tube in children is caused MOST often by

    A. adenoid growth around the nasal end of the tube
    B. deterioration in the inner ear
    C. ear wax
    D. perforation of the eardrum

4.____

5. It is generally agreed among authorities that a child should have training in lip reading when successive audiometric tests indicate that the better ear shows a LOSS of _____ decibels.

    A. 5   B. 10   C. 15   D. 25

5.____

6. The MOST satisfactory way to measure a patient for crutches is to have him

    A. stand against a wall, with his arms straight at side
    B. lie on his back, with his arms straight at side
    C. lie on his back, with his arms elevated over his head
    D. stand against a wall, with his arms extended over his head

6.____

7. In crutch walking, the weight is placed on the

    A. quadriceps muscle
    B. trapezius muscle
    C. deltoid muscle
    D. palms of the hands with wrists in hyperextension

7.____

8. If a nurse sees that a newborn holds his head to one side with his chin rotated in the opposite direction, she SHOULD recognize the condition as

    A. facial paralysis
    C. torticollis
    B. cerebral palsy
    D. cephalhematoma

8.____

9. Of the following types of cerebral palsy, the one which is characterized by tense con-   9._
tracted muscles is

    A. spastic   B. athetoid
    C. ataxic   D. dystonic

10. Of the following communicable diseases, the one that is characterized by the eruption of   10._
successive crops of rose pink spots which change into vesicles and finally into crusts is

    A. chicken pox   B. German measles
    C. scarlet fever   D. measles

11. The remarkable reduction in the incidence of typhoid fever is due PRIMARILY to   11._

    A. immunization
    B. control of human environment
    C. the use of antibiotics
    D. isolation of typhoid carriers

12. Antibodies which neutralize toxins are called   12._

    A. lysins   B. agglutinins
    C. antitoxins   D. opsonins

13. Brucellosis is USUALLY acquired in man by   13._

    A. direct contact with a human being having the disease
    B. direct contact with infected cattle
    C. ingestion of raw milk or milk products
    D. inhaling bacteria from the air

14. Immunity following successful vaccination against smallpox is now believed to last   14._

    A. for the lifetime of the individual
    B. at least seven years
    C. from one to three years
    D. a varying length of time from individual to individual

15. The gamma globulin fraction of pooled human plasma is an EFFECTIVE agent for pre-   15._
venting or modifying

    A. chicken pox   B. measles
    C. scarlet fever   D. diphtheria

16. Of the following, the one which is capable of ALTERING the course of tuberculosis is   16._

    A. streptomycin   B. B.C.G. vaccine
    C. the tuberculin test   D. the Schick test

17. Of the following, the FIRST symptom of spontaneous pneumothorax is   17._

    A. tightening of the chest with or without dyspnea
    B. acute dyspnea
    C. anxious expression of the face
    D. restlessness plus anxiety

18. To function effectively in the follow-up of a venereal disease patient, the one MOST important thing for the nurse to know is the   18.____

    A.   number of contacts the patient has had
    B.   correct medical diagnosis of the patient concerned
    C.   structure of the family
    D.   economic status of the family

19. The incubation period of neisseria gonorrhea is GENERALLY from _____ days.   19.____

    A.   3 to 6   B.   7 to 10
    C.   11 to 14   D.   15 to 18

20. Of the following, the one which prenatal syphilis SELDOM affects is the   20.____

    A.   nervous system   B.   spleen
    C.   liver   D.   heart

21. Even without treatment, a person infected with non-congenital syphilis is NOT dangerous to others after he has had the disease _____ months.   21.____

    A.   6   B.   12   C.   18   D.   2

22. In the treatment of syphilis, the antibiotic which has proven the MOST effective, with the LEAST toxic results, as well as the MOST economical, is   22.____

    A.   streptomycin   B.   aureomycin
    C.   penicillin   D.   chloromycetin

23. Of the following communicable diseases that may be contracted in the first trimester of pregnancy, the one which is BELIEVED to produce malformation in the newborn is   23.____

    A.   scarlet fever   B.   German measles
    C.   diphtheria   D.   measles

24. In the normal course of pregnancy, the total blood volume   24.____

    A.   decreases
    B.   increases and decreases at various times
    C.   remains normal
    D.   increases

25. In fetal growth, the period characterized by membranous nails and tooth buds occurs at the end of the _____ lunar month.   25.____

    A.   1st   B.   3rd   C.   5th   D.   7th

KEY (CORRECT ANSWERS)

1.	D		11.	B
2.	A		12.	C
3.	C		13.	C
4.	A		14.	D
5.	D		15.	B
6.	B		16.	A
7.	D		17.	A
8.	C		18.	B
9.	A		19.	A
10.	A		20.	D

21.	D
22.	C
23.	B
24.	D
25.	B

———

TEST 3

DIRECTIONS: Each question or incomplete statement is followed by several suggested answers or completions. Select the one that BEST answers the question or completes the statement. *PRINT THE LETTER OF THE CORRECT ANSWER IN THE SPACE AT THE RIGHT.*

1. The exercises included in the program of "natural childbirth" are PRIMARILY aimed at

    A. making the waiting time more interesting to the patient
    B. assuring the patient of a painless labor period
    C. relaxing the patient
    D. eliminating the use of anesthesia during labor

1._____

2. The UNDERLYING principle of "rooming in" for newborn infants and their mothers is that it

    A. prevents nursery infections in the baby
    B. requires less nursing time
    C. provides an opportunity for the mother to know and care for her baby while in the hospital
    D. encourages breast feeding

2._____

3. Erythroblastosis due to the RH factor in newborn infants MOST frequently results from

    A. transfusing an RH negative woman with RH positive blood
    B. the mating of an RH positive father and an RH negative mother
    C. the failure to determine the RH status of pregnant women
    D. transfusing the mother during pregnancy

3._____

4. A premature baby is BEST defined as an infant who

    A. is less than 9 months in gestation
    B. weighs 6 pounds at birth
    C. was born in the 7th month of gestation
    D. weighs 2500 grams or less at birth

4._____

5. Retrolental fibroplasia occurs in

    A. premature infants   B. pre-school children
    C. adolescents   D. old age

5._____

6. When advising a mother regarding infant feeding, the nurse should know that MOST pediatricians recommend that

    A. babies be fed when they cry
    B. mothers plan a three or four hour schedule and adhere to it without variation
    C. mothers need not adhere to a strict feeding schedule since each child has an individual feeding pattern which should be used as a guide
    D. infants never be fed more often than once every four hours

6._____

7. An average normal infant may FIRST be expected to sit alone at the age of _____ months.

    A. 5   B. 7   C. 9   D. 11

7._____

8. Of the following, the GREATEST single cause of infant and neonatal mortality is   8.__

    A. accidents   B. prematurity
    C. congenital malformation   D. pneumonia

9. Of the following statements relating to epilepsy, the one which is MOST correct is that   9.__

    A. epilepsy indicates feeblemindedness
    B. children with epilepsy should be treated as invalids
    C. seizures in about 50% of children with epilepsy can best be controlled with medicines now in use
    D. children with epilepsy should have permanent home teaching

10. The MOST rapid period of biological growth is during the _____ period.   10.__

    A. prenatal   B. pre-adolescent
    C. adolescent   D. post-adolescent

11. A nurse should advise a mother that bowel training is ORDINARILY successful   11.__

    A. at the same time as bladder training
    B. earlier than bladder training
    C. later than bladder training
    D. when the child is four months old

12. When cautioning about carbon monoxide poisoning, the nurse should recommend that the family   12.__

    A. keep a fire extinguisher handy at all times
    B. inspect gas, appliances daily
    C. keep a window open at least two inches in any room where there is a gas appliance
    D. do not inspect gas appliances with wet hands

13. In the treatment of severe burns, the FIRST consideration should be given to   13.__

    A. dressing the burned area
    B. treating for shock
    C. estimating the extent of the burned area
    D. giving large amounts of fluids

14. The FIRST step recommended in first aid treatment for an animal bite is   14.__

    A. cleansing the wound thoroughly with soap under running water
    B. application of any antiseptic solution
    C. application of tincture of iodine
    D. application of tincture of iodine followed by a band-aid

Questions 15-19.

DIRECTIONS: Next to Numbers 15 through 19, write the letter preceding the disease or condition mentioned in Column II which is most closely connected with the test mentioned in Column I, Numbers 15 through 19.

Column I	Column II	
15. Aschheim-Zondek	A. tuberculosis	15. ____
16. Dick	B. syphilis	16. ____
17. Kline	C. scarlet fever	17. ____
18. Mantoux	D. pregnancy	18. ____
19. Papanicolaou	E. diphtheria	19. ____
	F. diabetes	
	G. cancer	

Questions 20-25.

DIRECTIONS: Next to Numbers 20 through 25, write the letter preceding the term mentioned in Column II which is most closely connected with the definition given in Column I, Numbers 20 through 25.

Column I	Column II	
20. Inflammation of the kidneys	A. cretinism	20. ____
21. Alzeimer's disease	B. enuresis	21. ____
22. Involuntary passage of urine	C. geriatrics	22. ____
23. White blood corpuscle	D. leucocyte	23. ____
24. A form of idiocy and dwarfism	E. nephritis	24. ____
25. Lateral curvature of the spine	F. paraphasia	25. ____
	G. scoliosis	
	H. silicosis	

KEY (CORRECT ANSWERS)

1.	C		11.	B
2.	C		12.	C
3.	B		13.	B
4.	D		14.	A
5.	A		15.	D
6.	C		16.	C
7.	C		17.	B
8.	B		18.	A
9.	C		19.	G
10.	A		20.	E

21.	C
22.	B
23.	D
24.	A
25.	G

———

TEST 4

DIRECTIONS: Each question or incomplete statement is followed by several suggested answers or completions. Select the one that BEST answers the question or completes the statement. *PRINT THE LETTER OF THE CORRECT ANSWER IN THE SPACE AT THE RIGHT.*

1. The victim of a neck fracture should be transported   1.____

   A. face downward on a rigid support
   B. face upward on a rigid support
   C. lying on the left side of a rigid support
   D. sitting upright on a chair

2. Of the following, the PRIMARY cause of acne in adolescents is   2.____

   A. too much carbohydrate in the diet
   B. the inability of the fat gland ducts and outlets to allow passage of increased secre-
      tions of sebum
   C. lack of vitamin A in the diet
   D. lack of good personal hygiene

3. The nutritional needs of older people differ from those of young adults in that older peo-   3.____
   ple require MORE

   A. protein   B. minerals   C. calcium   D. calories

4. Planning for aging should be the responsibility CHIEFLY of   4.____

   A. the individual   B. the family
   C. industry   D. the total community

5. Prophylaxis against the diseases of old age is USUALLY directed toward   5.____

   A. preventing the onset of a disease
   B. preventing or minimizing the disability disease produces
   C. prohibiting all physical exercise
   D. providing for early retirement

6. Of the following, the MOST accurate statement with regard to the life expectancy of the   6.____
   diabetic today is that

   A. his life span is 1/3 that of the non-diabetic
   B. his life span approximates that of the non-diabetic, provided proper precautions are
      taken
   C. the diabetic seldom lives beyond age 60 because of complications which shorten
      life
   D. if diabetes occurs in childhood, the prognosis is good for a normal life span

7. N.P.H. insulin is generally considered the MOST valuable of the different types of insulin   7.____
   because it

   A. has a low protamine content as compared with protamine zinc insulin
   B. reaches its peak in eight hours, thus providing safety for the patient during the
      night

C. is well-adapted to the mild cases
D. meets the requirements of the greatest number of patients

8. When caring for elderly people with diabetes, it is MOST important for the nurse to   8.__

A. know that all diabetics must have insulin daily
B. understand their individual personalities and habits
C. teach them how to do urinalysis and give their own insulin
D. know that their diets require major adjustments

9. The GREATEST social problem affecting health which has increased in the past few   9.__
years is

A. juvenile delinquency
B. juvenile narcotic addiction
C. crowding of children in housing projects
D. migration of industrial workers

10. The MOST important reason for the nurse to keep records of patients is to   10.__

A. provide better service to the patients
B. give information to other agencies in the community
C. compile information for legal documents
D. keep *data* for tabulating vital statistics

11. The function of the nurse on a school health council is to   11.__

A. act in an advisory capacity to the principal and teaching staff in matters pertaining
to health
B. secure needed facilities for treatment of children with defects
C. plan the health education program for the school
D. organize the entire facilities of the school for the promotion of health

12. With regard to health services, the recommendation for enactment into law that was car-   12.__
ried out was that

A. the Children's Bureau be abolished
B. compulsory health insurance be inaugurated for all people in the United States
C. the Federal Security Agency be reorganized into a Department of Health, Educa-
tion and Welfare
D. the Children's Bureau and the United States Health Service be combined

13. If a nurse has been assigned the following four visits, all within a radius of a few blocks,   13.__
she should visit FIRST the case in which a(n)

A. anxious prenatal patient is going to be evicted from her home
B. school child was sent home from school because of Koplik spots
C. newborn baby is regurgitating every other feeding
D. newborn baby was discharged against the advice of the hospital to a home in
which the father has a positive sputum for tuberculosis

14. A nurse is assigned four visits. Of the following, the FIRST visit she should make is to a   14.____

    A. cardiac patient who receives mercuhydrin regularly twice a week
    B. patient receiving 20U. of N.P.H. insulin
    C. mother delivered of a baby by a non-nurse midwife at 4 A.M. that morning
    D. child sent home from school the previous day with a rash resembling scarlet fever

15. Assume that a mother expresses concern over her one-year-old baby's feeding habits.   15.____
As a nurse, you can BEST advise this mother by telling her that

    A. she should feed her baby, although he refuses to eat
    B. appetites of children begin to diminish at the end of the first year and continue to be small for a year or two
    C. poor eating habits in children are often a result of emotional problems between parents
    D. she should feed her child every two hours whether he is hungry or not

16. Assume that a nine-year-old boy comes to you for help. He has a splinter in his finger   16.____
which has been embedded for 24 hours and around which there is a reddened *area*.
The BEST course of action for you to take is to

    A. remove the splinter and apply an antiseptic solution
    B. wash the area with tincture of green soap, express gently, and apply an antiseptic solution
    C. have the boy soak his finger in hot water and instruct him to have his mother continue the soakings at home in order to loosen the splinter
    D. cover the area with a sterile dressing and call the mother to instruct her to take the child to a physician for treatment

17. A city of 100,000 reported 30 maternal deaths last year. Of the following, the statement   17.____
regarding the maternal death rate which is CORRECT is that it

    A. is 30%
    B. cannot be computed because we do not know the general death rate
    C. cannot be computed because we do not know the number of live births
    D. cannot be computed because we do not know the infant death rate

18. The agency which has as its objective "the attainment of the highest possible level of   18.____
health of all the people" is the

    A. American Red Cross
    B. World Health Organization
    C. United States Public Health Service
    D. The Children's Bureau

19. In the event of an atom bomb attack, civil defense authorities state that the one of the fol-   19.____
lowing which will cause the GREATEST number of deaths is

    A. radioactivity   B. injuries
    C. infections   D. hemorrhage

20. Insulin was isolated from other products of the pancreas by   20.____

    A. Louis Pasteur   B. Frederick Banting
    C. George Baker   D. Anton Von Leeuwenhoek

21. Recent studies indicate that the MOST economical and practical public health control method for dental caries is to

    A. promote a community-wide nutrition program
    B. provide community dental services for bi-yearly examination of school children
    C. provide individual daily fluoride supplements
    D. fluoridate the domestic water supply

22. During a poliomyelitis epidemic, of the following, the one precaution NOT recommended by the National Foundation for Infantile Paralysis is to

    A. keep clean
    B. avoid new groups
    C. avoid getting chilled
    D. keep children home from school

23. The LEADING cause of all deaths in the United States is

    A. cancer   B. diseases of infancy
    C. accidents   D. heart disease

24. The LEADING cause of school absences in the United States is

    A. accidents   B. skin diseases
    C. digestive disorders   D. respiratory infections

25. The National Cancer Institute established in the U.S. Public Health Service in 1937 has as its MAJOR goal

    A. research and dissemination of knowledge concerning the causes and treatment of cancer
    B. improving standards for the care of the cancer patient in both the home and hospital
    C. training of medical personnel in the treatment of cancer
    D. granting financial aid to states in the development of cancer control programs

KEY (CORRECT ANSWERS)

1.	B		11.	A
2.	B		12.	C
3.	C		13.	D
4.	D		14.	C
5.	B		15.	B
6.	B		16.	D
7.	D		17.	C
8.	B		18.	B
9.	B		19.	A
10.	A		20.	B

21.	D
22.	D
23.	D
24.	D
25.	D

———

EXAMINATION SECTION
TEST 1

DIRECTIONS: Each question or incomplete statement is followed by several suggested answers or completions. Select the one that BEST answers the question or completes the statement. *PRINT THE LETTER OF THE CORRECT ANSWER IN THE SPACE AT THE RIGHT.*

1. A nurse arrives in a home immediately after the birth of a premature baby for whom no preparation has been made. The MOST important factor to be considered in the immediate care of the baby is   1.____

    A. maintenance of body temperature
    B. removal to a hospital
    C. feeding with breastmilk
    D. demonstration of the infant's bath to the mother
    E. securing someone to give full-time care to the baby

2. The CHIEF cause of infant mortality is   2.____

    A. gastroenteritis   B. pneumonia
    C. prematurity   D. suffocation
    E. birth injuries

3. A child who carries the RH positive factor when his mother is an RH negative may develop a condition known as   3.____

    A. hypopituitarism   B. erythroblastosis
    C. autosomal genes   D. mongolism
    E. acromegaly

4. According to studies of child development, the one of the following behavior characteristics which you would expect to find in a normal two-year-old child is   4.____

    A. bladder control day and night
    B. ability to play well with a group
    C. ability to feed himself without help
    D. ability to converse in sentences
    E. ability to ride a tricycle

5. Authorities are agreed that the BEST time to begin training a child for bladder control is   5.____

    A. as soon as the mother observes a definite rhythm in urination
    B. when the child begins to walk
    C. not until the child can indicate verbally a desire to void
    D. at one year of age
    E. at nine months of age

6. In the age group 15 to 30, the one of the following diseases which is the CHIEF cause of death is   6.____

    A. puerperal sepsis   B. heart disease
    C. tuberculosis   D. syphilis
    E. appendicitis

7. In the age group 55 to 64, the one of the following diseases which is the CHIEF cause of death is   7.__

    A. circulatory disease   B. pneumonia
    C. tuberculosis   D. hemiplegia
    E. cancer

8. In 1976, the expectancy of life at birth had increased to about 61.5. This was a 20-year saving since 1900.   8.__
Of the following factors, the one to which MOST of this saving in life has been attributed is the

    A. improved living conditions, as a result of higher incomes
    B. effects of the discovery of bacteria
    C. increase in recreational facilities which has lowered nervous tension
    D. curtailment of arduous physical labor due to mechanical inventions
    E. federal, state, and municipal assistance to the indigent and the handicapped

9. The term *acquired immunity,* when used in connection with communicable disease, means the   9.__

    A. specific immunity developed as a result of a natural selection in a group of people living in any particular area
    B. immunity existing in an area where people have never contracted the disease
    C. immunity existing for a few months after birth given physiologically to the newborn baby by the mother
    D. specific immunity resulting from an attack of the disease or from artificial means
    E. immunity human beings have against certain diseases of lower animals

10. Children who have had rheumatic fever and, as a result, exhibit symptoms of heart disease, must be given special protection against   10.__

    A. exposure to acute communicable diseases
    B. cathartics which contain kidney irritants
    C. dietary fads to control weight
    D. sight and sounds which frighten them
    E. living in an enervating warm climate

11. A twenty-one-year-old man is found by x-ray to have minimal tuberculosis. The physician orders sanitorium care. Temporarily no beds are available.   11.__
The BEST advice the nurse can give in this instance until he can be admitted to the sanitorium is to

    A. encourage the man to visit a friend in Arizona.
    B. plan bed rest and isolation of the patient at home where his mother can care for him
    C. advise that he may continue work in his office position since the work is light and the lesion minimal
    D. encourage a seashore vacation where he may lie for hours in the sun
    E. advise an outdoor mountain vacation

12. The time of a well-prepared nurse in a busy syphilis clinic can BEST be used in   12.__

A. acting as receptionist to put patients at ease
B. giving intravenous treatments, thereby releasing the physicians to do physical examinations
C. taking histories and interpreting the disease and its treatment to patients
D. assisting the physician and taking notes on his physical examinations
E. managing the clinic smoothly so patients need not wait

13. The effect of syphilitic involvement of the eighth nerve in individuals with congenital syphilis is that it 13.____

A. usually causes facial paralysis, if the patient is not treated promptly
B. manifests itself very slowly and, therefore, may be easily controlled
C. is a relatively unimportant complication of the disease and responds readily to treatment
D. may be disregarded as a probable complication of the disease if the patient is over 6 years old
E. usually causes total deafness and is not readily responsive to treatment

14. The only way in which syphilis can be detected with CERTAINTY in pregnant women is by 14.____

A. actual discovery of active lesions, since in a new case the serology will remain negative until after parturition
B. a vaginal smear and dark-field examination, since in pregnancy the spirochetes migrate to the vagina mucosa
C. a careful case history, since recent discoveries indicate that serologic tests are non-specific in pregnancy
D. routine serologic tests, since the primary and secondary signs and symptoms are often repressed in pregnancy
E. the Rorschach test

15. The method which is GENERALLY recommended for preventing premature infant deaths resulting from inter-cranial hemorrhage is to 15.____

A. administer vitamin K to the mother before delivery and to the baby after birth
B. give the mother massive doses of calcium by hypodermic injection
C. increase the amount of codliver oil given to the mother so that the calcium is better utilized by the baby
D. give the infant parathyroid hormone in order to utilize available calcium
E. give the baby transfusions of gum tragacanth in normal saline

16. The MOST important factor in the control of breast cancer is 16.____

A. application of radium as soon as a lump appears in the breast
B. deep x-ray therapy of all suspected lipomas
C. biopsy of the glands in the axilla
D. operative intervention early in the disease
E. breastfeeding of infants as a preventive measure

17. Although there are still many unknown factors in the complete etiology of cancer, there is one to which authorities agree cancer can usually be validly attributed.
This factor is 17.____

A. the tendency to cancerous growths passed on in the chromosomes and genes
B. the mechanical action of finely divided airborne proteins
C. chronic irritation in various forms
D. degeneration of cells in the older age groups
E. the implantation, in some way yet unknown, of malignant growths

18. The type of tuberculosis that has been generalized as a result of the bacilli having been seeded into the bloodstream from a tuberculosis infection is   18.__

    A. miliary tuberculosis   B. tuberculosis meningitis
    C. tuberculosis enteritis   D. silicotic tuberculosis
    E. tuberculosis scrofula

19. The MOST common immediate cause of unsuccessful collapse of the lung by artificial pneumothorax is   19.__

    A. hemoptysis   B. cavitation
    C. pleurisy with effusion   D. caseous lesion
    E. pleural adhesions

20. A child is given the Mantoux test to detect the existence of tuberculosis infection. After three days, a raised edematous reddened area appears at the site of the test.   20.__
The CORRECT interpretation of the test result is:

    A. A primary infection is present which makes the child completely resistant to further exogenous infections
    B. The test shows evidence of infection, but does not indicate whether the process is active or quiescent
    C. The test shows evidence of active pulmonary tuberculosis
    D. The reaction may be due to protein sensitivity and a control test is required to eliminate this factor
    E. The child has been exposed to active tuberculosis, but has not acquired an infection

21. Of the following, the one which should receive the MOST emphasis by the school nurse in order to achieve the best results in improving school health education is   21.__

    A. classroom teaching in hygiene
    B. home visits to expand parent education
    C. assisting teachers to integrate health education in classroom teaching
    D. active participation in the health education programs of Parent-Teacher Associations
    E. parent education through group instruction at the time of the school health examination

22. A high school student is found to have a heart condition which warrants bed rest at home. Because only six weeks of the school term remain, the student wishes to complete the term, and is inclined to disregard the school physician's advice until the school term closes.   22.__
The BEST method the school nurse can take in handling this situation is to

A. visit the home to enlist the parents' cooperation and assist them in planning the necessary care, and encourage the student to follow the doctor's advice
B. discuss it with the school doctor and get his suggestions for adjustment in the school schedule to allow the student to complete the school term
C. refer the student to the Visiting Nurse Association for follow-up and instruction
D. advise the student that if she does remain in school to go to bed every day as soon as she gets home from school
E. advise the student to see her pharmacist for confirmation of the school physician's diagnosis

23. The one of the following criteria which is the BEST method for evaluating the success of the school health program is   23.____

A. improved health behavior as evidenced by the application of health knowledge in daily habits of living
B. an increased number of health classes in the school curriculum
C. the number of defects discovered and corrected in school children
D. the number of school children examined annually by their family physicians
E. an increased number of children entering school each year without defects

24. A kindgergarten school child is found by a visual acuity test to have 20/30 vision. The action the school nurse should take in this situation is to   24.____

A. send the child to an oculist for a complete eye examination
B. send a note to the child's parents advising that the child should wear glasses
C. do nothing since farsightedness is normal in young children
D. advise the teacher to reduce the amount of class work required of the child until the condition is corrected
E. enlist the cooperation of parents and teacher in teaching the child good eye hygiene

25. A nurse should know that blepharitis is a(n)   25.____

A. skin disease which is highly communicable
B. infection of the bladder
C. inflammation of the eyelids
D. disease caused by a fungus
E. nutritional deficiency disease

KEY (CORRECT ANSWERS)

1.	A	11.	B
2.	C	12.	C
3.	B	13.	E
4.	C	14.	D
5.	A	15.	A
6.	C	16.	D
7.	A	17.	C
8.	B	18.	A
9.	D	19.	E
10.	A	20.	B

21.	C
22.	A
23.	A
24.	E
25.	C

———

MEDICAL SCIENCE

EXAMINATION SECTION
TEST 1

DIRECTIONS: Each question or incomplete statement is followed by several suggested answers or completions. Select the one that BEST answers the question or completes the statement. *PRINT THE LETTER OF THE CORRECT ANSWER IN THE SPACE AT THE RIGHT.*

1. The one of the following which is a kidney operation is a   1.____

    A. gastrectomy   B. nephrectomy   C. lobectomy
    D. craniotomy   E. hysterectomy

2. The one of the following which is the medical term for nearsightedness is   2.____

    A. myopia   B. strabismus   C. hyperopia
    D. nystagmus   E. astigmatism

3. A patient with a Koch infection has   3.____

    A. gonorrhea   B. syphilis   C. cancer
    D. diabetes   E. tuberculosis

4. The one of the following which is the PRIMARY purpose of the Wasserman test taken during pregnancy is to   4.____

    A. prevent congenital symphilis
    B. find active cases of gonorrhea
    C. prevent infection of the husband
    D. prevent syphilis of the central nervous system
    E. prevent luetic heart disease

5. Diagnosing cancer in its early stages is important CHIEFLY because   5.____

    A. family members may be tested for hereditary predisposition
    B. chances of cure are greatest when treatment can begin early
    C. medication to prevent spread can be prescribed
    D. cancer can always be cured when treatment begins early
    E. the patient can be better isolated from contact with others

6. A cholecystectomy involves the removal of the   6.____

    A. thyroid   B. colon   C. liver
    D. gall bladder   E. spleen

7. A child has just recovered from acute rheumatic fever which has mildly affected his heart. The one of the following which is of GREATEST importance to him as a prophylactic measure is that   7.____

    A. his family be aware of the situation
    B. he attend a special class at school
    C. he have no stairs to climb
    D. he be on complete bed rest
    E. he take care to avoid colds

8. The one of the following conditions which is NOT mandatorily reportable to the Department of Health is   8.__

    A. smallpox   B. cancer   C. poliomyelitis
    D. syphilis   E. tuberculosis

9. The one of the following which represents the GREATEST value of special classes for children with marked eye defects is that   9.__

    A. there is less mental competition with normal children
    B. Braille books are made available to them
    C. sight conservation is taught and practiced
    D. corrective eye exercises are emphasized
    E. they can adjust better in the group

10. The one of the following diseases for which a sedimentation rate test is of GREATEST value is   10.__

    A. hyperthyroidism   B. rheumatic fever
    C. pneumonia   D. toxemia
    E. diabetes

11. Syphilis is caused by an infection with   11.__

    A. spirochaeta pallida   B. gram-negative diplocci
    C. tubercle bacilli   D. streptococci
    E. staphlylocci

12. The one of the following tests which is a basis for, or a confirmation of, a diagnosis of diabetes is a   12.__

    A. complete blood count
    B. darkfield examination
    C. spinal fluid examination
    D. patch test
    E. glucose tolerance test

13. The one of the following diseases which is caused by a deficiency of vitamin D is   13.__

    A. rickets   B. pellagra   C. beriberi
    D. scurvy   E. anemia

14. The one of the following diseases which has been MOST prevalent in the United States in the last five years is   14.__

    A. heart disease   B. typhoid   C. poliomyelitis
    D. tuberculosis   E. cancer

15. In establishing a diagnosis of pulmonary tuberculosis, the one of the following which is MOST valuable to the doctor is   15.__

    A. the Mantoux test   B. Roentgen study
    C. gastric lavago   D. a thermometer
    E. fluoroscopic study

16. The one of the following which is the MOST common cause of death from heart disease   16.____
in the age group of one week to five years is

    A. hypertension   B. angina pectoris
    C. syphilitic heart disease   D. congenital heart disease
    E. rheumatic heart disease

17. According to our present knowledge of the effects of certain diseases during the first   17.____
three months of pregnancy, the one of the following diseases which would have the
MOST harmful effect on the unborn fetus is

    A. German measles   B. gonorrhea
    C. heart disease   D. lobar pneumonia
    E. thrombophlebitis

18. According to the American Heart Association's classification, a 24-year-old female   18.____
patient classified as Functional, Class IA would be

    A. on complete bed rest
    B. warned against pregnancies
    C. allowed normal activity
    D. on a convalescent status
    E. restrained from any stair climbing

19. The one of the following diseases which is caused by a birth injury is   19.____

    A. cerebral palsy   B. meningitis
    C. hydrocele   D. congenital syphilis
    E. epilepsy

20. In helping a patient who has arteriosclerotic heart disease to plan for his future, the one   20.____
of the following phases on which you would specifically seek information from the
patient's doctor is the

    A. emotional basis of the illness
    B. etiology of the disease process
    C. functioning capacity of the patient
    D. awareness of hereditary predisposition
    E. anatomical changes which have occurred

21. The one of the following eye conditions which is MOST commonly found in the premature   21.____
infant is

    A. strabismus   B. myopia
    C. phylctenular keratitis   D. retrolental fibroplasia
    E. glaucoma

22. The one of the following cases in which eclampsia is MOST likely to occur is   22.____

    A. diabetes   B. shock therapy
    C. syphilitic infection   D. measles
    E. pregnancy

23. A delusion is a   23.____

    A. disharmony of mind and body
    B. fantastic image formed during sleep

C. false judgment of objective things
D. cessation of thought
E. distorted perception or image

24. The one of the following which is the MOST common form of treatment employed by psychiatrists in treating patients with mental disorders is
  24.__

  A. hypnotism
  B. hydrotherapy
  C. electroshock
  D. insulin shock
  E. psychotherapy

25. A masochistic person is one who
  25.__

  A. is very melancholy
  B. has delusions of grandeur about himself
  C. derives pleasure from being cruelly treated
  D. believes in a fatalistic philosophy
  E. derives pleasure from hurting another

26. Surgery is ESPECIALLY difficult during the oedipal period because of the
  26.__

  A. father attachment
  B. mental age
  C. castration anxieties
  D. rejection complex
  E. separation from siblings

27. A psychometric test is one which attempts to measure
  27.__

  A. social adjustment
  B. emotional maturity
  C. physical activity
  D. personality development
  E. intellectual capacity

28. The one of the following conditions which falls into the classification of a psychosis rather than psychoneurosis is
  28.__

  A. anxiety hysteria
  B. schizophrenia
  C. neurasthenia
  D. conversion hysteria
  E. compulsion neurosis

29. The one of the following which BEST describes psychosomatic medicine is
  29.__

  A. the understanding and treatment of both mind and body in illness
  B. the treatment of disease by psychiatric methods only
  C. the separation of mind and body in medical treatment
  D. the psychological testing of all individuals
  E. a system of socialized medical planning

30. The one of the following conditions for which shock treatment is FREQUENTLY used is
  30.__

  A. alcoholism
  B. Parkinson's syndrome
  C. multiple sclerosis
  D. schizophrenia
  E. diabetes

31. The incidence of any particular disease is called the _____ rate.
  31.__

  A. mortality
  B. morbidity
  C. endemic
  D. death
  E. differential

32. The one of the following which is the PRIMARY purpose of the mass chest x-ray surveys   32._____
    is to

    A. find active cases of tuberculosis
    B. give early treatment for tuberculosis
    C. educate the public
    D. lower the death rate among the aged
    E. carry out a research project

33. When a child develops whooping cough after having been closely exposed to the dis-   33._____
    ease, the cause is said to be

    A. endogenous   B. exogenous   C. endemic
    D. endoglobular   E. ectatic

34. The one of the following diseases for which the necessary medication will be given free   34._____
    by the Department of Health is

    A. poliomyelitis   B. pneumonia   C. cancer
    D. syphilis   E. epilepsy

35. The branch of medical science which deals with the conditions of the older age group is   35._____
    called

    A. pediatrics   B. dietetics   C. gerontology
    D. orthopedics   E. cardiology

KEY (CORRECT ANSWERS)

1.	B		16.	D
2.	A		17.	A
3.	E		18.	C
4.	A		19.	A
5.	B		20.	C
6.	D		21.	D
7.	E		22.	E
8.	B		23.	C
9.	C		24.	E
10.	B		25.	C
11.	A		26.	C
12.	E		27.	E
13.	A		28.	B
14.	A		29.	A
15.	B		30.	D

31.	B
32.	A
33.	B
34.	D
35.	C

TEST 2

DIRECTIONS: Each question or incomplete statement is followed by several suggested answers or completions. Select the one that BEST answers the question or completes the statement. *PRINT THE LETTER OF THE CORRECT ANSWER IN THE SPACE AT THE RIGHT.*

1. Eclampsia is MOST likely to occur in the course of

   A. pregnancy   B. poliomyelitis
   C. German measles   D. scarlet fever

1.__

2. The one of the following diseases which is characterized by an overabundance of white cells in the body is

   A. hemophilia   B. polycythemia
   C. anemia   D. leucemia

2.__

3. The GREATEST single factor in improving the prognosis in diabetes in children is

   A. improvement in standards of living
   B. the discovery of insulin
   C. greater emphasis on prenatal care
   D. improved surgical techniques

3.__

4. The one of the following which FREQUENTLY causes a baby to be cyanotic at birth is

   A. a neurological disorder   B. congenital heart disease
   C. gonorrhea   D. tuberculosis

4.__

5. In establishing a diagnosis of *grand mal,* the one of the following which would be MOST helpful to the doctor is an(the)

   A. electrocardiogram
   B. encephalogram
   C. basal metabolism rate
   D. blood pressure reading

5.__

6. Oophorectomy is a surgical procedure involving removal of the

   A. kidney   B. brain lobe
   C. ovary   D. thyroid gland

6.__

7. The one of the following laboratory procedures which is used SPECIFICALLY in diagnosing cancer is a

   A. glucose tolerance test   B. dark-field examination
   C. blood test   D. Papanicolaou smear

7.__

8. Cerebral palsy is known as _____ disease.

   A. Pott's   B. Little's   C. Addison's   D. Grave's

8.__

9. An electroencephalogram is used in establishing a diagnosis of

   A. rheumatic heart disease   B. cholecystitis
   C. Hodgkin's disease   D. epilepsy

9.__

10. The one of the following conditions which is NOT caused by the dysfunction of endocrine glands is   10._____

    A. myxedema   B. duodenal ulcer
    C. cretinism   D. Addison's disease

11. A diagnostic procedure used in determining the presence of syphilis is a   11._____

    A. patch test   B. dark-field examination
    C. sputum test   D. gastric analysis

12. An eye condition necessitating the use of glasses which COMMONLY appears with the advent of middle age is   12._____

    A. myopia   B. strabismus
    C. presbyopia   D. fibroplasia

13. The one of the following laboratory tests which is performed to determine or confirm the presence of central nervous system syphilis is a   13._____

    A. glucose tolerance test   B. sedimentation test
    C. colloidal gold test   D. Papanicolaou smear

14. A COMMON surgical procedure used in the treatment of duodenal ulcer is   14._____

    A. nephrectomy   B. cholecystectomy
    C. lobectomy   D. subtotal gastrectomy

15. The one of the following tests which is used to determine the presence of dysfunction of the thyroid gland is   15._____

    A. a sputum test   B. an electroencephalogram
    C. gastric analysis   D. a basal metabolism test

16. The MOST effective antibiotic in present-day treatment of syphilis is   16._____

    A. penicillin   B. streptomycin
    C. terramycin   D. aureomycin

17. The one of the following which is COMMONLY used to determine the presence of a brain tumor is   17._____

    A. a cardiogram   B. urinalysis
    C. a glucose tolerance test   D. a ventriculogram

18. Under the Sanitary Code, it is necessary to report the positive results of certain tests or specimen examinations to the Department of Health within 24 hours.
The one of the following which does NOT have to be reported is   18._____

    A. a positive Zondek-Aschheim test
    B. the presence of Klebs-Loeffler bacilli
    C. the presence of bacillus typhosus
    D. a positive Kline-Young test

19. A curette is a   19._____

    A. healing drug   B. curved scalpel
    C. long hypodermic needle   D. scraping instrument

20. A myocardial infarct would occur in the   20.___

    A. heart   B. kidneys   C. lungs   D. spleen

Questions 21-25.

DIRECTIONS: For Questions 21 through 25, Column I lists body organs and Column II lists names of surgical procedures. For each body organ listed in Column I, select the surgical procedure in Column II which involves the organ, and write the letter which precedes the surgical procedure in the answer blank corresponding to the number of the question.

<u>COLUMN I</u>

21. Brain

22. Gall bladder

23. Larynx

24. Reproductive organs

25. Stomach

<u>COLUMN II</u>

A. Cholecystectomy   21.___

B. Enucleation   22.___

C. Gastrectomy   23.___

D. Lobotomy   24.___

E. Nephrectomy   25.___

F. Orchidectomy

G. Tracheotomy

KEY (CORRECT ANSWERS)

1.	A		11.	B
2.	D		12.	C
3.	B		13.	C
4.	B		14.	D
5.	B		15.	D
6.	C		16.	A
7.	D		17.	D
8.	B		18.	A
9.	D		19.	D
10.	B		20.	A

21.	D
22.	A
23.	G
24.	F
25.	C

EXAMINATION SECTION
TEST 1

DIRECTIONS: Each question or incomplete statement is followed by several suggested answers or completions. Select the one that BEST answers the question or completes the statement. *PRINT THE LETTER OF THE CORRECT ANSWER IN THE SPACE AT THE RIGHT.*

1. Multiphasic screening, now adopted by many health departments, is BEST defined as a   1.____

    A. new method of testing vision
    B. case finding procedure combining tests for several diseases
    C. combined vision and hearing test
    D. new method of cancer detection

2. Of the following statements that a nurse might make to a patient ill with cancer who says,   2.____
I don't think I'll ever get better. When the pain comes, I'm afraid I'll die before anyone gets here, the one which would be MOST appropriate is:

    A. I wouldn't worry about that. People do not die because of pain.
    B. Of course you'll get better. You look much better than you did the last time I was here.
    C. You should try to have someone here with you and not be alone. Then you won't be afraid.
    D. I think I understand how you feel, but why do you think you won't get better?

3. In an epidemiological study of a disease, the one of the following steps which would usu-   3.____
ally NOT be included is

    A. collecting and compiling data on the incidence, prevalence, and trends of the disease
    B. reviewing the *natural history* of the disease
    C. making a sociological study of the community in which the disease is prevalent
    D. defining gaps in knowledge and developing hypotheses on which to base further investigation

4. Adequate lighting in the school is an important part of the sight conservation program.   4.____
The school nurse familiar with standards for classroom lighting should know that the RECOMMENDED illumination on each desk for ordinary classroom work is _____ candles.

    A. 20-foot   B. 35-foot   C. 50-foot   D. 75-foot

5. The relation of fluorine to dental health has been the subject of extensive study for many   5.____
years.
Of the following statements concerning the relation of fluorine to dental caries, the one which is CORRECT is that

    A. mass medication by fluorine is now accepted as the best means of treating and curing dental caries
    B. fluoridation of water supplies, though effective, is too expensive for wide usage
    C. fluoridation is effective only in children born in areas in which fluoridation exists
    D. fluoridation prevents dental caries but does not treat or cure it

6. There are measures which are effective in the prevention of diabetes in those with an hereditary disposition.
Of the following, the one which has the GREATEST value as a preventive measure is

    A. preventing acute infection
    B. preventing obesity
    C. avoidance of emotional stress
    D. avoidance of marriage with a known diabetic

6._

7. The basis of a program of *natural childbirth* is to

    A. prevent or dispel fear through education in the physiology of pregnancy
    B. reduce premature births and the complications of pregnancy
    C. reduce the maternal and neonatal mortality rates
    D. prepare the mother's body for the muscular activity of delivery

7._

8. The one of the following statements which is CORRECT concerning retrolental fibroplasia is that it is a

    A. blood dyscrasia
    B. condition occurring in Rh negative infants whose mothers are Rh positive
    C. condition causing blindness in premature infants
    D. complication of congenital syphilis

8._

9. Of the following factors, the one which is MOST important in maintaining optimum health in the older age group is

    A. regular medical supervision for early recognition and treatment of minor symptoms
    B. economic independence which gives a feeling of security
    C. avoidance of all emotional tensions
    D. adjustment of the environment to prevent physical and mental strain

9._

10. The MOST outstanding result of antibiotic therapy in the treatment of syphilis has been to

    A. reduce the toxic effect of treatment
    B. shorten the treatment period
    C. prevent a relapse
    D. prevent late complications

10._

11. To achieve the most effective and economical case finding for tuberculosis, mass examinations should be conducted PRIMARILY for

    A. infants under one year
    B. industrial workers
    C. elementary school students
    D. pre-school age group

11._

12. Though tuberculosis occurs in all age groups, there is a certain period of life when individuals have the greatest resistance to the infection.
That period is

    A. under one year of age
    B. between 3 years and puberty
    C. between 15 and 35 years of age
    D. between 25 and 40 years of age

12._

13. Drug therapy for tuberculosis has proven to be an important tool in the control of the dis-   13._____
ease in its active stage.
Of the following, the one which has had the MOST satisfactory results to date in that
fewer patients develop resistance to the drug and the incidence of drug toxicity is
reduced is

    A. para-amino-salicylic acid (P.A.S.) in combination with streptomycin
    B. dihydro-streptomycin
    C. streptomycin in combination with promine
    D. penicillin

14. Studies have indicated that the use of streptomycin in the treatment of tuberculosis has   14._____
GREATEST value in

    A. recently developed pneumonic or exudative lesions
    B. long standing infections which have been resistant to other therapies
    C. military T.B.
    D. meningeal T.B.

15. The PARTICULAR effectiveness of chemotherapeutic agents in the treatment of pulmo-   15._____
nary tuberculosis is that they

    A. are important adjuncts to surgery
    B. inhibit the growth of the bacillus
    C. heal lesions rapidly
    D. render the patient non-infectious

_____

KEY (CORRECT ANSWERS)

1.	B		6.	B
2.	D		7.	A
3.	C		8.	C
4.	A		9.	A
5.	D		10.	B

11.	B
12.	B
13.	A
14.	A
15.	B

_____

TEST 2

DIRECTIONS: Each question or incomplete statement is followed by several suggested answers or completions. Select the one that BEST answers the question or completes the statement. *PRINT THE LETTER OF THE CORRECT ANSWER IN THE SPACE AT THE RIGHT.*

1. The CHIEF shortcoming of chemotherapeutic agents in the treatment of pulmonary tuberculosis is

   A. their prohibitive cost in any long-term treatment
   B. the toxic effects which follow their use
   C. that their use is limited to early cases
   D. the development of bacterial resistance by the host

1.___

2. Though precise knowledge concerning the optimum duration of chemotherapy in treating pulmonary tuberculosis is lacking, the present APPROVED practice is

   A. continued uninterrupted treatment until the sputum is negative
   B. short courses of treatment with rest periods in between
   C. continued treatment for a minimum of 12 months
   D. continued treatment for one year after a negative sputum and cultures are obtained

2.___

3. A community program for the control of tuberculosis must include school children and school personnel if it is to be a success.
   Of the following statements, the one which BEST represents expert opinion on the use of B.C.G. vaccine in the school program for tuberculosis control is that

   A. through immunization of all school children it serves as an important control measure
   B. its chief value is that it is an inexpensive and rapid method of case finding
   C. it would nullify the subsequent use of the tuberculin test which is the best case finding method for schools
   D. it is a valuable diagnostic method which would reduce the evidence of contact with active cases

3.___

4. Nutritional deficiencies are a common problem in geriatrics.
   The dietary adjustment usually necessary to maintain PROPER nutrition for the average person in the older age group is

   A. increased proteins and vitamins
   B. elimination of fats
   C. increased carbohydrates
   D. elimination of roughage

4.___

5. The death rate from cancer can be reduced by early diagnosis and treatment. It is important, therefore, for the nurse to assist in case finding.
   She should know that, of the following sites, the one which the GREATEST incidence of cancer in women occurs is the

   A. mouth   B. skin   C. breast   D. rectum

5.___

6. Many cancers appear to develop when pre-existing abnormal conditions and changes in the tissue are present.
Of the following, the one which is at present considered PRECANCEROUS is

    A. fibroid tumor   B. chronic cervicitis
    C. fat tissue tumor   D. sebaceous cyst

6.____

7. The diagnosis of cancer by examination of isolated cells in body secretions is known as

    A. biopsy   B. aspiration technique
    C. histological diagnosis   D. Papanicolaou smear

7.____

8. Of the following statements concerning our present knowledge of the etiology of human cancer, the one which is TRUE is that

    A. there is definite evidence that some cancers are caused by a virus
    B. some types of cancer are definitely contagious
    C. there is a strong possibility that cancer is transmitted from mother to baby in utero
    D. so many factors are involved that the discovery of a single cause is unlikely

8.____

9. The National Venereal Disease Control Program carried on by the Public Health Service of the U.S. Government is concerned PRIMARILY with

    A. promoting medical programs to provide early effective treatment of infected individuals
    B. a national program of education in the prevention of venereal diseases
    C. distribution of free drugs to physicians for the treatment of venereal disease
    D. providing funds for the education of physicians and nurses in the treatment and care of venereal disease

9.____

10. Of the following, the one which is of GREATEST importance in the prevention of poliomyelitis is to

    A. build up resistance with proper diet
    B. keep away from crowds during periods when the disease is prevalent
    C. immunize with gamma globulin
    D. adopt general public health measures for the protection of food and water

10.____

11. Of the following statements concerning the present status of chemotherapy in the treatment of cancer, the one which is TRUE is:

    A. Results to date indicate it may soon surpass radiation and surgery as an effective cure
    B. It has not proven effective except in cases where early diagnosis was made
    C. It must be used in conjunction with radiation or surgery
    D. It inhibits the growth of certain types of cancer and prolongs life but is not effective as a cure

11.____

12. The W.H.O. Regional Organization for Europe has set up a long-term plan for European health needs.
Of the following activities, the one which is NOT planned as a major activity is

12.____

A. coordinating health policies in European countries
B. promoting improved service through demonstration of an ideal health program in one country
C. promoting professional and technical education for health workers in the member countries
D. providing for exchange of services among member nations

13. A health problem becomes the concern of public health authorities when the incidence is great and the mortality rate high.
In terms of this statement, of the following problems, the one which should be a PRIMARY concern is

A. venereal diseases in young adults
B. tuberculosis
C. tropical diseases among ex-servicemen and their families
D. degenerative diseases of middle and later life

13.__

14. Of the following, the one which is now considered to be the MOST common mode of transmission of poliomyelitis is

A. infected insects
B. contaminated water
C. personal contact
D. infected food

14.__

15. The incubation period for infantile paralysis is

A. usually 7 to 14 days, but may vary from 3 to 35 days
B. not known
C. one week
D. usually 48 hours, but may vary from 1 to 7 days

15.__

KEY (CORRECT ANSWERS)

1.	D	6.	B
2.	C	7.	D
3.	C	8.	D
4.	A	9.	A
5.	C	10.	B

11.	D
12.	B
13.	D
14.	C
15.	A

EXAMINATION SECTION
TEST 1

DIRECTIONS: Each question or incomplete statement is followed by several suggested answers or completions. Select the one that BEST answers the question or completes the statement. *PRINT THE LETTER OF THE CORRECT ANSWER IN THE SPACE AT THE RIGHT.*

Questions 1-15.

DIRECTIONS: In the following questions numbered 1 through 15, the word in capitals is the name of an anatomical part which is a segment of a larger structure or system For each question, select the letter preceding the structure or system of which the word in capitals is a part.

1. ESOPHAGUS   1.____

    A.   circulatory system   B.   bronchi
    C.   submaxillary   D.   respiratory system

2. ALVEOLI   2.____

    A.   nervous system   B.   lungs
    C.   endocrine system   D.   muscle

3. DELTOID   3.____

    A.   upper arm   B.   rib cage
    C.   circulatory system   D.   superior vena cava

4. FEMORAL ARTERY   4.____

    A.   right ventricle   B.   left auricle
    C.   circulatory system   D.   lymphatic system

5. BRACKIAL PLEXUS   5.____

    A.   circulatory system   B.   nervous system
    C.   respiratory system   D.   bronchi

6. ERYTHROCYTE   6.____

    A.   lymph glands   B.   skeletal system
    C.   blood   D.   large intestine

7. STERNUM   7.____

    A.   spinal column   B.   muscular system
    C.   nervous system   D.   skeletal system

8. THYMUS   8.____

    A.   endocrine system   B.   pituitary gland
    C.   parathyroids   D.   adrenals

9. MANDIBLE   9.____

    A. pelvis   B. head   C. liver   D. stomach

10. PECTORAL   10.___

    A. skeletal system   B. patella
    C. chest   D. digestive tract

11. CORNEA   11.___

    A. arm   B. eye   C. blood   D. lymph

12. CRANIUM   12.___

    A. circulatory system   B. left auricle
    C. skeletal system   D. abdomen

13. TRAPEZIUS   13.___

    A. breastbone   B. muscular system
    C. endocrine system   D. spinal column

14. MEGALOBLAST   14.___

    A. blood   B. pelvis   C. spleen   D. head

15. ADRENAL   15.___

    A. mouth   B. respiratory system
    C. liver   D. endocrine system

Questions 16-25.

DIRECTIONS: The following questions numbered 16 through 25 are concerned with various categories of diseases. For each question, select the letter preceding the disease or condition which MOST properly belongs to the category listed.

16. BONE DISEASE   16.___

    A. arrhythmia   B. arthritis
    C. edema   D. gastritis

17. DISEASE OF THE DIGESTIVE SYSTEM   17.___

    A. diabetes   B. osteomyelitis
    C. ileitis   D. conjunctivitis

18. DISEASE OF THE RESPIRATORY SYSTEM   18.___

    A. cyanosis   B. poliomyelitis
    C. jaundice   D. bronchiectasis

19. DISEASE OF THE HEART   19.___

    A. hepatitis   B. influenza
    C. encephalitis   D. myocarditis

20. DISEASE OF THE BLOOD   20.___

    A. leukemia   B. diphtheria
    C. pneumonia   D. colitis

21. NUTRITIONAL DISEASE   21.____

    A. hyperemia   B. mononucleosis
    C. trichinosis   D. scurvy

22. DISEASE OF THE NERVOUS SYSTEM   22.____

    A. amebiasis   B. parkinsonism
    C. ascariasis   D. tapeworm

23. PARASITIC DISEASE   23.____

    A. salmonella   B. neuralgia
    C. hemophilia   D. bursitis

24. SKIN DISEASE   24.____

    A. hydrocephalus   B. leprosy
    C. adenitis   D. angina

25. DISEASE OF THE URINARY TRACT   25.____

    A. myasthenia gravis   B. colitis
    C. hydronephrosis   D. dermatitis

KEY (CORRECT ANSWERS)

1.	D		11.	B
2.	B		12.	C
3.	A		13.	B
4.	C		14.	A
5.	B		15.	D
6.	C		16.	B
7.	D		17.	C
8.	A		18.	D
9.	B		19.	D
10.	C		20.	A

21. D
22. B
23. A
24. B
25. C

TEST 2

DIRECTIONS: Each question or incomplete statement is followed by several suggested answers or completions. Select the one that BEST answers the question or completes the statement. *PRINT THE LETTER OF THE CORRECT ANSWER IN THE SPACE AT THE RIGHT.*

Questions 1-10.

DIRECTIONS: Questions 1 through 10 are concerned with various categories of diseases. For each question, select the letter preceding the disease or condition which MOST properly belongs to the category listed.

1. DISEASE OF THE HEART   1.___

    A. diabetes   B. tachycardia
    C. osteoporosis   D. adenitis

2. SKIN DISEASE   2.___

    A. cholelithiasis   B. colitis
    C. psoriasis   D. encephalitis

3. DISEASE OF THE BLOOD   3.___

    A. polycythemia   B. ileitis
    C. psoitis   D. dermatitis

4. DISEASE OF THE RESPIRATORY SYSTEM   4.___

    A. dysentery   B. angina
    C. hemophilia   D. pneumonia

5. DISEASE OF THE DIGESTIVE SYSTEM   5.___

    A. periastitis   B. bronchiectasis
    C. enteritis   D. pertussis

6. PARASITIC DISEASE   6.___

    A. ascariasis   B. nephritis
    C. hyperemia   D. neuralgia

7. NUTRITIONAL DISEASE   7.___

    A. entasis   B. pellagra
    C. amebiasis   D. diphtheria

8. BONE DISEASE   8.___

    A. gangrene   B. epilepsy
    C. osteochondritis   D. bronchitis

9. DISEASE OF THE NERVOUS SYSTEM   9.___

    A. mononucleosis   B. gallstones
    C. jaundice   D. multiple sclerosis

10. DISEASE OF THE URINARY TRACT   10._____

    A. hydrocephalus   B. glomerulonephritis
    C. cyanosis   D. bursitis

Questions 11-25.

DIRECTIONS: For the following questions 11 through 25, select the letter preceding the part or system of the body which is CHIEFLY affected by the disease in capitals.

11. CONJUNCTIVITIS   11._____

    A. ear   B. intestines
    C. eye   D. liver

12. EMPHYSEMA   12._____

    A. heart   B. bronchial tubes
    C. pancreas   D. lymph nodes

13. CHOLELITHIASIS   13._____

    A. muscles   B. liver
    C. bones   D. common bile duct

14. PYELONEPHRITIS   14._____

    A. intestinal tract   B. arterial walls
    C. ligaments   D. urinary tract

15. EPILEPSY   15._____

    A. nervous system   B. pancreas
    C. thyroid   D. stomach

16. DYSENTERY   16._____

    A. tendons   B. kidneys
    C. intestines   D. brain

17. ERYTHROBLASTOSIS   17._____

    A. kidneys   B. blood
    C. endocrine system   D. large intestine

18. GLAUCOMA   18._____

    A. blood vessels   B. cortex
    C. cerebellum   D. eye

19. OSTEOPOROSIS   19._____

    A. bones   B. central nervous system
    C. adrenals   D. lymph nodes

20. MENINGITIS   20._____

    A. nasal passages   B. intestinal tract
    C. spinal cord   D. urinary tract

21. BURSITIS   21.__

    A. urinary tract   B. bones
    C. nasal passages   D. heart

22. ENDOCARDITIS   22.__

    A. cortex   B. kidneys   C. pancreas   D. heart

23. DIVERTICULOSIS   23.__

    A. thyroid   B. endocrine system
    C. intestinal tract   D. kidneys

24. ENCEPHALITIS   24.__

    A. brain   B. vessels   C. kidneys   D. eye

25. ILEITIS   25.__

    A. nervous system   B. blood
    C. liver   D. intestinal tract

KEY (CORRECT ANSWERS)

1.	B	11.	C
2.	C	12.	B
3.	A	13.	D
4.	D	14.	D
5.	C	15.	A
6.	A	16.	C
7.	B	17.	B
8.	C	18.	D
9.	D	19.	A
10.	B	20.	C

21.	B
22.	D
23.	C
24.	A
25.	D

EXAMINATION SECTION
TEST 1

DIRECTIONS: Each question or incomplete statement is followed by several suggested answers or completions. Select the one that BEST answers the question or completes the statement. *PRINT THE LETTER OF THE CORRECT ANSWER IN THE SPACE AT THE RIGHT.*

Questions 1-20.

DIRECTIONS: Column I below lists words used in medical practice. Column II lists phrases which describe the words in Column I. Opposite the number preceding each of the words in Column I, place the letter preceding the phrase in Column II which BEST describes the word in Column I.

COLUMN I   COLUMN II

1. Abrasion

2. Aseptic

3. Cardiac

4. Catarrh

5. Contamination

6. Dermatology

7. Disinfectant

8. Dyspepsia

9. Epidemic

0. Epidermis

1. Incubation

2. Microscope

3. Pediatrics

4. Plasma

5. Prenatal

6. Retina

7. Syphilis

8. Syringe

9. Toxemia

0. Vaccine

A. A disturbance of digestion

B. Destroying the germs of disease

C. A general poisoning of the blood

D. An instrument used for injecting fluids

E. A scraping off of the skin

F. Free from disease germs

G. An apparatus for viewing internal organs by means of x-rays

H. An instrument for assisting the eye in observing minute objects

I. An inoculable immunizing agent

J. The extensive prevalence in a community of a

K. Chemical product of an organ

L. Preceding birth

M. Fever

N. The branch of medical science that relates to the skin and its diseases

O. Fluid part of the blood

P. The science of the hygienic care of children

Q. Infection by contact

R. Relating to the heart

S. Inner structure of the eye

T. Outer portion of the skin

U. Pertaining to the ductless glands

V. An infectious venereal disease

W. The development of an infectious disease from the period of infection to that of the appearance of the first symptoms

X. Simple inflammation of a mucous membrane

Y. An instrument for measuring blood pressure

1.____

2.____

3.____

4.____

5.____

6.____

7.____

8.____

9.____

10.____

11.____

12.____

13.____

14.____

15.____

16.____

17.____

18.____

19.____

20.____

Questions 21-25.

DIRECTIONS: Each of Questions 21 through 25 consists of four words. Three of these words belong together. One word does NOT belong with the other three. For each group of words, you are to select the one word which does NOT belong with the other three words.

21. A. conclude   B. terminate   C. initiate   D. end   21

22. A. deficient   B. inadequate   22
     C. excessive   D. insufficient

23. A. rare   B. unique   C. unusual   D. frequent   23

24. A. unquestionable   B. uncertain   24
     C. doubtful   D. indefinite

25. A. stretch   B. contract   C. extend   D. expand   25

KEY (CORRECT ANSWERS)

1.	E	11.	W
2.	F	12.	H
3.	R	13.	P
4.	X	14.	O
5.	Q	15.	L
6.	N	16.	S
7.	B	17.	V
8.	A	18.	D
9.	J	19.	C
10.	T	20.	I

21.	C
22.	C
23.	D
24.	A
25.	B

TEST 2

DIRECTIONS: Each question or incomplete statement is followed by several suggested answers or completions. Select the one that BEST answers the question or completes the statement. *PRINT THE LETTER OF THE CORRECT ANSWER IN THE SPACE AT THE RIGHT.*

Questions 1-4.

DIRECTIONS: Questions 1 through 4 pertain to the meaning of terms which may be encountered in laboratory work. For each question, select the option whose meaning is MOST NEARLY the same as that of the numbered item.

1. Atrophied   1._____

    A. enlarged   B. relaxed
    C. strengthened   D. wasted

2. Leucocyte   2._____

    A. white cell   B. red cell
    C. epithelial cell   D. dermal cell

3. Permeable   3._____

    A. volatile   B. variable
    C. flexible   D. penetrable

4. Attenuate   4._____

    A. dilute   B. infect
    C. oxidize   D. strengthen

Questions 5-11.

DIRECTIONS: For Questions 5 through 11, select the letter preceding the word which means MOST NEARLY the same as the first word.

5. legible   5._____

    A. readable   B. eligible   C. learned   D. lawful

6. observe   6._____

    A. assist   B. watch   C. correct   D. oppose

7. habitual   7._____

    A. punctual   B. occasional
    C. usual   D. actual

8. chronological   8._____

    A. successive   B. earlier
    C. later   D. studious

9. arrest   9.___

    A. punish   B. run   C. threaten   D. stop

10. abstain   10.___

    A. refrain   B. indulge   C. discolor   D. spoil

11. toxic   11.___

    A. poisonous   B. decaying
    C. taxing   D. defective

12. The *initial* contact is of great importance in setting a pattern for future relations.   12.___
    The word *initial,* as used in this sentence, means MOST NEARLY

    A. first   B. written   C. direct   D. hidden

13. The doctor prescribed a diet which was *adequate* for the patient's needs.   13.___
    The word *adequate,* as used in this sentence, means MOST NEARLY

    A. insufficient   B. unusual
    C. required   D. enough

14. The child was reported to be suffering from a vitamin *deficiency.*   14.___
    The word *deficiency,* as used in this sentence, means MOST NEARLY

    A. surplus   B. infection   C. shortage   D. injury

15. In obtaining medical case data, a medical record librarian should discourage the patient   15.___
    from giving *irrelevant* information.
    The word *irrelevant,* as used in this sentence, means MOST NEARLY

    A. too detailed   B. pertaining to relatives
    C. insufficient   D. inappropriate

16. The doctor requested that a *tentative* appointment be made for the patient.   16.___
    The word *tentative,* as used in this sentence, means MOST NEARLY

    A. definite   B. subject to change
    C. later   D. of short duration

17. The black plague resulted in an usually high *mortality rate* in the population of Europe.   17.___
    The term *mortality rate,* as used in this sentence, means MOST NEARLY

    A. future immunity of the people
    B. death rate
    C. general weakening of the health of the people
    D. sickness rate

18. The public health assistant was asked to file a number of *identical* reports on the case.   18.___
    The word *identical,* as used in this sentence, means MOST NEARLY

    A. accurate   B. detailed   C. same   D. different

19. The nurse assisted in *the biopsy* of the patient.   19.____
    The word *biopsy,* as used in this sentence, means MOST NEARLY

    A. autopsy
    B. excision and diagnostic study of tissue
    C. biography and health history
    D. administering of anesthesia

20. The assistant noted that the swelling on the patient's face had *subsided.*   20.____
    The word *subsided,* as used in this sentence, means MOST NEARLY

    A. become aggravated   B. increased
    C. vanished   D. abated

21. The patient was given food *intravenously.*   21.____
    The word *intravenously,* as used in this sentence, means MOST NEARLY

    A. orally   B. against his will
    C. through the veins   D. without condiment

Questions 22-25.

DIRECTIONS: Each of Questions 22 through 25 consists of four words. Three of these words
            belong together. One word does NOT belong with the other three. For each
            group of words, you are to select the one word which does NOT belong with
            the other three words.

22. A. accelerate   B. quicken   C. accept   D. hasten   22.____

23. A. sever   B. rupture   C. rectify   D. tear   23.____

24. A. innocuous   B. injurious C. dangerous   D. harmful   24.____

25. A. adulterate   B. contaminate   25.____
    C. taint   D. disinfect

KEY (CORRECT ANSWERS)

1. D	11. A	21. C
2. A	12. A	22. C
3. D	13. D	23. C
4. A	14. C	24. A
5. A	15. D	25. D
6. B	16. B	
7. C	17. B	
8. A	18. C	
9. D	19. B	
10. A	20. D	

TEST 3

Questions 1-25.

1. TEMPORARY   1.___

    A. permanently   B. for a limited time
    C. at the same time   D. frequently

2. INQUIRE   2.___

    A. order   B. agree   C. ask   D. discharge

3. SUFFICIENT   3.___

    A. enough   B. inadequate
    C. thorough   D. capable

4. AMBULATORY   4.___

    A. bedridden   B. left-handed
    C. walking   D. laboratory

5. DILATE   5.___

    A. enlarge   B. contract   C. revise   D. restrict

6. NUTRITIOUS   6.___

    A. protective   B. healthful
    C. fattening   D. nourishing

7. CONGENITAL   7.___

    A. with pleasure   B. defective
    C. likeable   D. existing from birth

8. ISOLATION   8.___

    A. sanitation   B. quarantine
    C. rudeness   D. exposure

9. SPASM   9.___

    A. splash   B. twitch   C. space   D. blow

10. HEMORRHAGE   10.____

    A. bleeding   B. ulcer
    C. hereditary disease   D. lack of blood

11. NOXIOUS   11.____

    A. gaseous   B. harmful   C. soothing   D. repulsive

12. PYOGENIC   12.____

    A. disease producing   B. fever producing
    C. pus forming   D. water forming

13. RENAL   13.____

    A. brain   B. heart   C. kidney   D. stomach

14. ENDEMIC   14.____

    A. epidemic
    B. endermic
    C. endoblast
    D. peculiar to a particular people or locality, as a disease

15. MACULATION   15.____

    A. reticulation   B. inoculation
    C. maturation   D. defilement

16. TOLERATE   16.____

    A. fear   B. forgive   C. allow   D. despise

17. VENTILATE   17.____

    A. vacate   B. air   C. extricate   D. heat

18. SUPERIOR   18.____

    A. perfect   B. subordinate
    C. lower   D. higher

19. EXTREMITY   19.____

    A. extent   B. limb   C. illness   D. execution

20. DIVULGED   20.____

    A. unrefined   B. secreted   C. revealed   D. divided

21. SIPHON   21.____

    A. drain   B. drink   C. compute   D. discard

22. EXPIRATION   22.____

    A. trip   B. demonstration
    C. examination   D. end

23. AEROSOL   23.___

    A.   a gas dispersed in a liquid
    B.   a liquid dispersed in a gas
    C.   a liquid dispersed in a solid
    D.   a solid dispersed in a liquid

24. ETIOLOGY   24.___

    A.   cause of a disease   B.   method of cure
    C.   method of diagnosis   D.   study of insects

25. IN VITRO   25.___

    A.   in alkali   B.   in the body
    C.   in the test tube   D.   in vacuum

KEY (CORRECT ANSWERS)

1.	B		11.	B
2.	C		12.	C
3.	A		13.	C
4.	C		14.	D
5.	A		15.	D
6.	D		16.	C
7.	D		17.	B
8.	B		18.	D
9.	B		19.	B
10.	A		20.	C

21.	A
22.	D
23.	B
24.	A
25.	C

BASIC NURSING PROCEDURES:
FUNDAMENTAL NURSING CARE OF THE PATIENT

TABLE OF CONTENTS

BASIC NURSING PROCEDURES: FUNDAMENTAL NURSING CARE OF THE PATIENT

1. MORNING CARE

PURPOSE

To refresh and prepare patient for breakfast.

EQUIPMENT

Basin of warm water
Towel, washcloth and soap
Toothbrush and dentifrice/mouthwash
Curved basin
Glass of water
Comb

PROCEDURE

1. Clear bedside stand or overbed table for food tray.
2. Offer bedpan and urinal.
3. Wash patient's face and hands.
4. Give oral hygiene.
5. Place patient in a comfortable position for breakfast.
6. Comb hair.

POINTS TO EMPHASIZE

1. Morning care is given before breakfast by night corpsman.
2. Assist handicapped, aged or patients on complete bed rest.

CARE OF EQUIPMENT

Wash, dry and replace equipment.

———

2. ORAL HYGIENE

PURPOSE

To keep mouth clean.
To refresh patient.
To prevent infection and complications in the oral cavity.
To stimulate appetite.

EQUIPMENT

Glass of water
Curved basin
Toothbrush and dentifrice - electric toothbrush if available
Mouth wash
Towel
Drinking tubes as necessary

PROCEDURE

1. A patient who is able to help himself:
    a. Place patient in comfortable position.
    b. Arrange equipment on bedside table within his reach.

2. A patient who needs assistance:
    a. Place patient in comfortable position.
    b. Place towel under his chin and over bedding.
    c. Moisten brush, apply dentifrice and hand to the patient.
    d. Hold curved basin under his chin while he cleanses his teeth and mouth.
    e. Remove basin. Wipe lips and chin with towel.

POINTS TO EMPHASIZE

Oral hygiene is particularly important for patients
    a. who are not taking food and fluid by mouth
    b. with nasogastric tubes
    c. with productive coughs
    d. who are receiving oxygen therapy

CARE OF EQUIPMENT

Wash equipment with soap and hot water, rinse, dry and put away.

---

3. SPECIAL MOUTH CARE

PURPOSE

To cleanse and refresh mouth.
To prevent infection.

EQUIPMENT

Electric toothbrush if available
Tray with:
Mineral oil or cold cream
Lemon-glycerine applicators
Paper bag
Drinking tubes or straws
Applicators and gauze sponges
Curved basin
Paper wipes
Bulb syringe

Cleansing agents

Tooth paste
Equal parts of hydrogen peroxide and water
Mouthwash

Glass of water
Suction machine for unconscious patient

PROCEDURE

1. Tell patient what you are going to do.
2. Turn patient's head to one side.
3. Brush teeth and gums.
4. When it is not possible to brush teeth and gums, moisten applicator with a cleansing agent and use for cleaning oral cavity and teeth.
5. Assist patient to rinse mouth with water.
6. If patient is unable to use drinking tube, gently irrigate the mouth with a syringe directing the flow of water to side of mouth.
7. Apply lubricant to lips.

For Unconscious Patient

Use suction machine.

SPECIAL MOUTH CARE (Continued)

POINTS TO EMPHASIZE

1. Extreme care should be exercised to prevent injury to the gums.
2. Position patient carefully to prevent aspiration of fluids.
3. Caution patient not to swallow mouthwash.

CARE OF EQUIPMENT

Dispose of applicator and soiled gauze. Clean equipment and restock tray.

———

4. CARE OF DENTURES

PURPOSE

To aid in keeping mouth in good condition.
To cleanse the teeth.

EQUIPMENT

Container for dentures
Toothbrush and dentifrice
Glass of water
Mouthwash
Curved basin
Towel
Paper towels

PROCEDURE

1. Have patient rinse mouth with mouthwash.
2. Remove dentures. Place them in container.
3. Have patient brush tongue and gums with mouth-wash.
4. Place a basin under tap in sink and place paper towels in basin. Fill basin with cold water.
5. Hold dentures over basin and under cold running water. Wash with brush and dentifrice.
6. Place dentures in container of cold water. Take to patient's bedside.
7. Replace wet dentures.

POINTS TO EMPHASIZE

1. Handle dentures carefully to prevent breakage.
2. When not in use, dentures should be placed in covered container of cold water and placed in top drawer of locker.
3. Give special attention to the inner surfaces of clips used to hold bridge work or partial plates in place.

CARE OF EQUIPMENT

Wash equipment, rinse, dry and put away.

5. BED BATH

PURPOSE

To cleanse the skin.
To stimulate the circulation.
To observe the patient mentally and physically.
To aid in elimination.

EQUIPMENT

Linen and pajamas as required
Half filled basin of water
Bar of soap
Rubbing alcohol/skin lotion
Bedpan and urinal with cover
Bed screens

PROCEDURE

1. Tell patient what you are going to do.
2. Screen patient.
3. Offer bedpan and urinal.
4. Shave patient or allow patient to shave himself.
5. Lower backrest and knee rest if physical condition permits.
6. Loosen top bedding at foot and sides of bed.
7. Remove pillow and place on chair.
8. Remove and fold bedspread and blanket. Place on back of chair.
9. Remove pajamas and place on chair.
10. Assist patient to near side of bed.
11. Bathe the patient:

    a. Eyes:
       (1) Do not use soap.
       (2) Clean from inner to outer corner of eye.

    b. Face, neck and ears.
    c. Far arm.
    d. Place hand in basin and clean nails.
    e. Near arm.
    f. Place hand in basin and clean nails.
    g. Chest.
    h. Abdomen.

BED BATH (Continued)

PROCEDURE (Continued)

12.

      i.   Far leg, foot and nails. Place foot in basin when possible.
      j.   Near leg, foot and nails. Place foot in basin when possible.
      k.   Change water. l. Back and buttocks.
      m.   Genitals and rectal area.

13. Give back rub.
14. Put on pajamas.
15. Comb hair.
16. Make bed.
17. Adjust bed to patient's comfort unless contrain-dicated.

POINTS TO EMPHASIZE

1. Give bed baths daily and P.R.N.
2. Give oral hygiene before bath.
3. Avoid drafts which might cause chilling.
4. Use bath towel under all parts to aid in keeping the bed linen as dry as possible.
5. Change bath water after washing lower extremities and as necessary.
6. Be sure all soap film is rinsed from body to prevent skin irritation.
7. Keep patient well draped at all times.
8. Observe and chart the condition of the skin in regard to lesions, rashes and reddened areas.
9. Pillow should be removed unless contraindicated to give patient a change of position.
10. Assist handicapped patients with shaving.
11. Always move or turn patient toward you.

CARE OF EQUIPMENT

1. Remove soiled linen and place in hamper.
2. Wash equipment, rinse, dry and put away.

6. <u>MAKING AN UNOCCUPIED BED</u>

<u>PURPOSE</u>

To provide a clean, comfortable bed.
To provide a neat appearance to the ward.

<u>EQUIPMENT</u>

Two sheets
Plastic mattress cover
Blanket
Plastic pillow cover
Pillowcase
Protective draw sheet or disposable pads, if indicated

<u>PROCEDURE</u>

1. Place mattress cover on mattress. Where necessary and available, plastic mattress covers are used.
2. Place center fold of sheet in center of bed, narrow hem even with foot of bed.
3. Fold excess sheet under the mattress at head of bed.
4. Miter corner.
   a. Pick up hanging sheet 12 inches from head of bed.
   b. Tuck lower corner under mattress.
   c. Bring triangle down over side of bed.
   d. Tuck sheet under mattress.
5. Pull bottom sheet tight and tuck under side of mattress.
6. If draw sheets are indicated, place in center of bed as illustrated. Tuck excess under mattress.
   a. Linen draw sheet is made by folding a regular bed sheet in half - hem to hem.
7. Place center fold of second sheet in center of bed, with hem even with the top of mattress.
8. Tuck excess under foot of mattress.
9. Center fold blanket in middle of bed 6 inches from top of mattress.
10. Fold excess under foot of mattress.
11. Make mitered corner.

MAKING AN UNOCCUPIED BED (Continued)

PROCEDURE (Continued)

12. Place bedspread on bed, center fold in middle of bed even with the top of the mattress. Fold under blanket.
13. Fold cuff of top sheet over bedspread at head of bed.
14. Tuck excess spread under foot of mattress.
15. Miter corner at foot of mattress.
16. Go to other side of bed and follow steps 3 to 15.
17. Place plastic cover on pillow.
18. Place pillow case on pillow.
19. Place pillow on bed with seams at head of bed, open end away from the entrance to the ward.

POINTS TO EMPHASIZE

1. Woolen blankets are to be used only when cotton blankets are not available.
2. Never use woolen blankets when oxygen therapy is in use.
3. Use protective draw sheet or protective pads when indicated.

MITERED CORNER

Pick up hanging sheet 12 inches from head of bed.

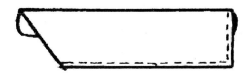

Tuck lower corner under mattress.

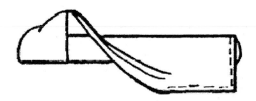

Bring triangle down over side of bed.

Tuck sheet under mattress.

COMPLETING FOUNDATION
APPLY DRAW SHEETS

1. PLACE RUBBER DRAW SHEET IN CENTER OF BED

2. TUCK EXCESS RUBBER DRAW SHEET IN ON NEAR SIDE OF MATTRESS

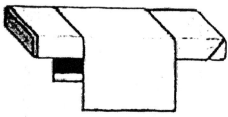

3. PLACE COTTON DRAW SHEET OVER RUBBER DRAW SHEET

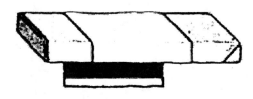

4. TUCK EXCESS COTTON DRAW SHEET IN ON NEAR SIDE OF MATTRESS

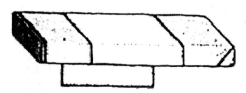

5. TUCK EXCESS RUBBER DRAW SHEET IN ON OPPOSITE SIDE OF MATTRESS

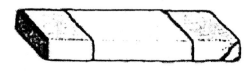

6. TUCK EXCESS COTTON DRAW SHEET IN ON OPPOSITE SIDE OF MATTRESS

7. MAKING AN OCCUPIED BED

PURPOSE

To provide clean linen with least exertion to patient.
To refresh patient.
To prevent pressure sores.

EQUIPMENT

Two sheets
Pillowcase
Blanket
Protective draw sheet or disposable pads, if indicated
Hamper

PROCEDURE

1. Place chair at foot of bed.
2. Push bedside locker away from bed.
3. Pull mattress to head of bed.
4. Loosen all bedding.
5. Remove pillow and place on chair.
6. Remove bedspread by folding from top to bottom, pick up in center and place on back of chair.
7. Remove blanket in same manner.
8. Turn patient to one side of the bed.
9. If cotton draw sheet is used, roll draw sheet close to patient's back.
10. Turn back protective sheet over patient.
11. Roll bottom sheet close to patient's back.
12. Straighten mattress cover as necessary.
13. Place clean sheet on bed with the center fold in the middle and narrow hem even with foot of bed.
14. Tuck in excess at head of bed. Miter corner and tuck in at side.
15. Bring down protective sheet; straighten and tuck in.
16. Make draw sheet by folding a sheet from hem to hem with smooth side out.
17. Place on bed with fold toward head of bed. Tuck in.

MAKING AN OCCUPIED BED (Continued)

PROCEDURE (Continued)

18. Roll patient over to completed side of bed.
19. Go to other side of the bed.
20. Remove soiled sheets and place in hamper.
21. Check soiled linen for personal articles.
22. Turn back draw sheets over patient.
23. Pull bottom sheet tight and smooth.
24. Pull protective sheet and draw sheet tight and smooth.
25. Bring patient to center of bed.
26. Place top sheet over patient, wide hem even with top of mattress.
27. Ask patient to hold clean top sheet.
28. Remove soiled top sheet. Place in hamper.
29. Place blanket 6 inches from top of mattress.
30. Make pleat in sheet and blanket over patient's toes.
31. Tuck in excess at foot of bed and miter corners.
32. Place bedspread on bed even with top of mattress. Fold under blanket.
33. Fold sheet over bedspread and blanket at head of bed.
34. Tuck in excess bedspread at foot of bed. Miter corners. Allow triangle to hang loosely.
35. Put clean pillowcase on pillow. Place under patient's head with closed end toward entrance to ward.
36. Adjust bed as desired by patient.
37. Straighten unit. Leave bedside stand within reach of patient.

POINTS TO EMPHASIZE

1. Always turn patient toward you to prevent possibility of injury and/or falls.
2. Make sure that foundation sheets are smooth and dry.

———————

MAKING AN OCCUPIED BED

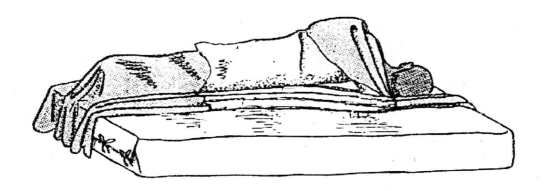

TURN PATIENT TOWARD YOU
FAN FOLD SOILED LINEN
AGAINST PATIENTS BACK

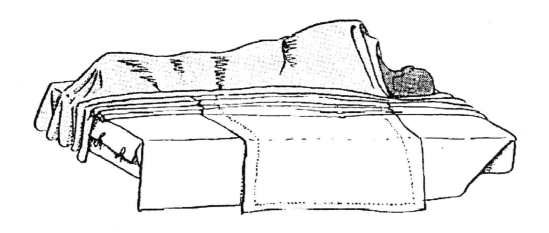

MAKE UP ONE HALF THE BED
BOTTOM SHEET, THEN
RUBBER DRAW SHEET

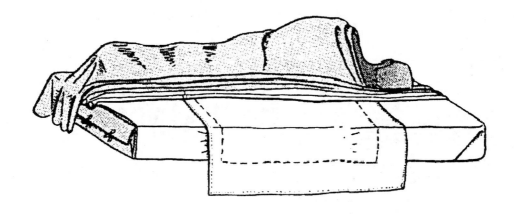

ADD COTTON DRAW SHEET

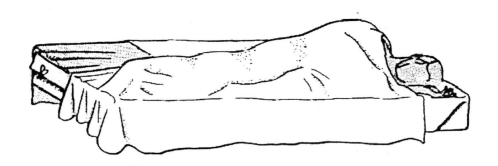

TURN PATIENT ONTO CLEAN LINEN
MAKE OPPOSITE SIDE OF BED

8. SERVING DIETS FROM FOOD CART

PURPOSE

To provide an attractively served food tray for a patient in a hospital where central food tray service is not available.

EQUIPMENT

Cart with food
Cart with trays, dishes, silver, and serving utensils

PROCEDURE

1. Clear the patient's bedside or overbed table.
2. Place table within patient's reach.
3. Place patient in a comfortable position.
4. Wash hands. Wheel food and tray carts to the unit.
5. Place beverage, salad, soup and dessert on the tray.
6. Fill glasses, cups and bowls three fourths full.
7. Serve small portions of hot food in an attractive manner.
8. Check diet list for type of diet each patient is to receive.
9. Carry tray and place it in a convenient position for the patient. Help the patient with the food if necessary.
10. After patient has finished, note how much he has eaten. Collect tray and return to main galley.

POINTS TO EMPHASIZE

1. The ward should be quiet and in readiness for meals.
2. Serve hot food hot and cold food cold.
3. Ice cream, sherbert and jello are kept in the refrigerator until ready to serve.
4. Do not hurry patient.
5. Do not smoke while working with food.
6. Refer to Special Diet Manual for special diet information.
7. Check visible file to determine if patient may have regular diet.
8. Make rounds to check that every patient has been served and received the correct diet.

SERVING DIETS FROM FOOD CART (Continued)

CARE OF EQUIPMENT WHERE MAIN GALLEY DOES NOT HAVE DISH WASHING FACILITIES

1. Scrape and stack dishes:
   a. Solid food into garbage can.
   b. Liquids into drain.
2. Clean and stack trays.
3. Wash dishes with hot soapy water. Stack in dish sterilizer.
4. Follow instructions on sterilizer. Temperature of final rinse water 180° F. Allow to air dry. Put away.
5. Place trays on cart with tray cover, silver and napkins. Salt, pepper, sugar go on all trays except Special Diets.
6. Clean food cart. Return to main galley.

9. CENTRAL TRAY SERVICE

PURPOSE

To provide attractively served food to the patient in an efficient manner.

PROCEDURE

1. Check list of patients who are not permitted food or fluids by mouth.
2. Clear bedside or overbed table.
3. Place table within reach of patient.
4. Place patient in comfortable position.
5. Wash hands. Wheel cart with trays to unit.
6. Take tray from cart and check to see if it is complete.
7. Read tray card.
8. See that tray is served to patient listed on the selective menus or the Special Diet Request that is placed on each tray.
9. Call each patient by name or check his identification band. Place his tray within easy reach.
10. Feed patient or assist him as necessary such as buttering his bread, cutting his meat, etc. Allow patient to do as much for himself as possible.
11. Make rounds to check that each patient entitled to a tray has been fed. The Diet List may be used as a check off list.
12. After the patient has finished eating, collect tray immediately and return to cart. Make a note of food eaten and record on Intake and Output Sheet as indicated.
13. Report all complaints about food to Food Service.

POINTS TO EMPHASIZE

1. Serve trays promptly.
2. Do not hurry patient.
3. Make rounds to check that all patients have been fed.

10. CARE OF ICE MACHINE AND HANDLING OF ICE, BEDSIDE PITCHERS, AND GLASSES

PURPOSE

To prevent ice machines from becoming a source of infection due to cross-contamination.

EQUIPMENT

To clean and disinfect ice machine:
Clean gloves, disposable
4x4 sponges
Scouring powder
Sodium hypochlorite
Clean 1 gallon container
Clean ice scoop

PROCEDURE

1. Disconnect ice machine from electrical outlet.
2. Wash hands.
3. Use ice scoop to dispose of any existing ice. Pour tap water into ice storage compartment to melt any remaining ice.
4. Put on gloves and remove scale and other debris with 4x4 sponges and scouring powder.
5. Rinse thoroughly with tap water.
6. Place 1/2 ounce of sodium hypocholrite in 1 gallon of water.
7. Using 4 x 4's wipe all accessible areas of interior with sodium hypochlorite solution. Pay particualr attention to ice chute.
8. Repeat step #7.
9. Allow solution to remain in machine for 30 minutes.
10. Rinse thoroughly with clean tap water three times.
11. Clean the exterior of the ice machine.
12. Connect ice machine to electrical outlet.

POINTS TO EMPHASIZE

1. Keep exterior of machine clean between weekly disinfecting of interior.
2. Limit access to ice machine to nursing service personnel.
3. Always keep door closed when not removing ice.
4. Locate ice machine in a "clean" area of the ward or hospital.
5. If ice must be transported, containers should be clean and covered.
6. Use a scoop or tongs when handling ice. Never handle ice with bare hands.
7. Never store the scoop in the ice when not in use.

CARE OF ICE MACHINE AND HANDLING OF
ICE, BEDSIDE PITCHERS, AND GLASSES (Continued)

POINTS TO EMPHASIZE (Continued)

8. The scoop or tongs must be sanitized at least daily.
9. Each patient should have his own bedside water pitcher with cover.
10. Glasses used for drinking water should be sent to the kitchen for exchange of clean glasses on a routine basis.
11. Culture ice machines according to local hospital policy and record in ice culture log.

CARE OF EQUIPMENT

1. Discard disposable equipment.
2. Replace cleaning gear.

11. FEEDING THE HELPLESS PATIENT

PURPOSE

To promote adequate nutrition of the helpless patient.
To encourage self-help when condition permits.

PROCEDURE

1. Place the patient in a sitting position unless otherwise ordered.
2. Place a towel across the patient's chest. Tuck a napkin under his chin.
3. Place tray on overbed table or bedside stand.
4. Give the patient a piece of buttered bread if he is able to hold it.
5. Feed the patient in the order in which he likes to be fed,
6. Offer liquids during the meal. Have patient use a drinking tube if necessary.
7. Give a small amount of food at one time. Allow the patient to chew and swallow food before offering him more. Do not rush your patient.
8. If patient is inclined to talk, talk with him.
9. Note amount of food he has taken. Record amount of fluid if on measured intake and output.
10. Remove tray. Leave patient comfortable.

POINTS TO EMPHASIZE

1. As you are feeding a blind patient tell him what you are offering and whether it is hot or cold.
2. Encourage a blind patient to begin feeding himself as soon as he is able and when indicated.
3. When encouraging a blind patient to feed himself, arrange tray the same way each time. Place foods on plate in the same clockwise direction and fill glasses and cups one-half full to avoid spilling.
4. If patient has difficulty in swallowing, have oral suction machine at bedside.

12. EVENING CARE

PURPOSE

To relax and prepare patient for the night.
To observe the patient's condition.

EQUIPMENT

Basin of warm water
Towel, washcloth and soap
Toothbrush, and dentifrice/mouthwash
Curved basin
Glass of water
Rubbing alcohol/skin lotion
Comb

PROCEDURE

1. Offer bedpan and urinal.
2. Give oral hygiene.
3. Wash patient's face and hands.
4. Wash back. Give back rub. Comb hair.
5. Straighten and tighten bottom sheets.
6. Freshen pillows.
7. Place extra blanket at foot of bed if weather is cool.
8. Make provision for ventilation of unit.
9. Clean and straighten unit and remove excess gear.

POINTS TO EMPHASIZE

1. Indicated for all bed patients and those on limited activity.
2. Change soiled linen as necessary.
3. Patient may assist with care as condition permits.
4. Ask the patient if soap may be used on the face.
5. Screen patients who require the use of bedpan.

13. CARE OF THE SERIOUSLY ILL PATIENT

PURPOSE

To provide optimum care and close observation of the seriously ill patient.
To keep the patient mentally and physically comfortable.

EQUIPMENT

Special mouth care tray
Rubbing alcohol/skin lotion
Bed linen as necessary
Pillow and/or supporting appliances
Special equipment as needed:

I.V. Standard
Suction machine
Oxygen
Drainage bottles
Intake and Output work sheet

PROCEDURE

1. Place patient where he can be easily and <u>closely</u> observed.
2. Keep room quiet, clean and clear of excess gear.
3. Bathe patient daily and P.R.N.
4. Maintain good oral hygiene every 2-4 hours.
5. Wash, rub back and change position every 2 hours unless contraindicated.
6. Speak to patient in a calm, natural tone of voice even if he appears to be unconscious.
7. Report any sudden change in condition.
8. Keep an accurate intake and output record if ordered.
9. Offer fluids if patient is conscious and is able to take them.
10. Record and Report:
    a. Changes in T.P.R. and blood pressure.
    b. State of consciousness.
    c. All observations.

CARE OF THE SERIOUSLY ILL PATIENT (Continued)

POINTS TO EMPHASIZE

1. All patients are seen by a chaplain when they are placed on the Serious or Very Seriously ill list.
2. Be considerate and kind to the patient's relatives.
3. Keep charting up-to-date.
4. Do not discuss patient's condition when the conversation might be overheard by the patient or unauthorized persons.
5. Refer all questions concerning the patient's condition to the doctor or nurse.
6. Be sure all procedures for placing a patient on the SL or VSL have been completed; for exmaple, inventory of personal effects and valuables.

———

BASIC NURSING PROCEDURES:
TAKING TEMPERATURE, PULSE, AND BLOOD PRESSURE

CONTENTS

BASIC NURSING PROCEDURES:
TAKING TEMPERATURE, PULSE, AND BLOOD PRESSURE

I. TAKING ORAL TEMPERATURE
A. THERMOMETERS DISINFECTED ON WARD

PURPOSE

To determine the patient's body temperature as recorded on a clinical thermometer.

EQUIPMENT

1. Tray containing:
   a. Two containers of disinfecting agent marked #1 and #2
   b. Container of green soap solution
   c. Container of water
   d. Container of clean cotton
   e. Waste container for soiled cotton
   f. Minimum of 6 thermometers, 3 in each container of disinfecting solution
   g. T.P.R. book
   h. Pencil and pen
   i. Watch with second hand

PROCEDURE

1. Take equipment to bedside.
2. Tell the patient what you are going to do.
3. Remove thermometer from container #1.
4. Wipe thermometer (over waste container) with water moistened sponge from stem to bulb using rotary motion. Discard sponge in waste container.
5. Shake down thermometer mercury to 95° F.
6. Place thermometer under patient's tongue. Caution him to keep his lips closed.
7. Distribute other thermometers to second and third patients in same manner.
8. Take third patient's pulse and respiration. Record results in T.P.R. book.
9. Take pulse and respiration of second patient, record, then first patient. Record results in T.P.R. book.
10. Remove thermometer from first patient's mouth after 3 minutes.
11. Wash thermometer (over waste container) with soap-moistened sponge from stem to bulb using rotary motion. Discard sponge in waste container.

PROCEDURE (Continued)

12. Moisten cotton sponge with water and wipe thermometer from stem to bulb in a rotary container. Discard sponge in waste container.
13. Read thermometer. Record results in T.P.R. book.
14. Place thermometer in the <u>original</u> container of disinfecting agent.
15. Repeat the steps 10 through 13 for second and third patients.
16. Disinfect these thermometers for a minimum of 20 minutes (depending on disinfecting agent used).
17. Continue using thermometers from alternate containers until all patient's temperatures have been taken.
18. Record T.P.R.'s on SP 511.

CARE OF EQUIPMENT

1. After each use
   a. Remove waste.
   b. Clean tray.
   c. Reset tray.
   d. Replace solutions (water - soap).
2. Daily
   a. Wash containers in warm, soapy water, rinse and dry.
   b. Change all solutions.
   c. Wash thermometers in cold, soapy water, rinse and place in disinfecting agent.
   d. Refill and reset tray.

POINTS TO EMPHASIZE

1. Wait for 10 minutes before taking temperature of patient who has had hot or cold drink or who has been smoking.
2. Be sure thermometer reads 95 or below before using it.
3. Encircle abnormal vital signs with red pencil in T.P.R. book.
4. Report all abnormal vital signs to Charge Nurse.
5. Describe quality of pulse and respiration in the observation column on Nursing Notes (SF 510).

POINTS TO EMPHASIZE (Continued)

6. After washing thermometer with soap, be sure to rinse well with water before putting it into disinfectant, as bacterial action is nullified in the presence of soap; for example, Zephiran chloride and iodine preparations.
7. Individual thermometers should be used for patients suspected of having a communicable disease.

THERMOMETERS STERILIZED IN CENTRAL SUPPLY ROOM

EQUIPMENT

1. Tray containing:
   a. Container of sterile oral thermometers that are sealed in paper envelopes.
   b. Container of green soap solution.
   c. Container of clean cotton.
   d. Container for waste material.
   e. T.P.R. book.
   f. Pencil.
   g. Watch with second hand.

PROCEDURE

1. Tell the patient what you are going to do.
2. Remove thermometer from envelope.
3. Shake thermometer mercury to 95° F.
4. Place thermometer under patient's tongue. Caution him to keep his lips closed.
5. Take, record and report vital signs as in previous procedure, numbers 7 through 11, pages 25 and 26.

CARE OF EQUIPMENT

1. After each use:
   a. Empty container of waste cotton.
   b. Return container of soiled thermometers to CSR in accordance with local instructions and exchange for an adequate supply of clean thermometers.
   c. Reset tray.
2. Daily:
   a. Wash containers in warm, soapy water, rinse and dry.
   b. Refill and reset tray.

———

TAKING ORAL TEMPERATURE
B. INDIVIDUAL THERMOMETER TECHNIQUE

PURPOSE

To determine the patient's body temperature as recorded on a clinical thermometer.

EQUIPMENT

1. Individual thermometer for each patient at bedside
2. Plastic thermometer holder with disinfectant solution - protective container of 2 1/2 cc. disposable syringe can be used
3. Adhesive tape
4. Container of clean cotton balls
5. Container for soiled cotton balls
6. T.P.R. book and pen
7. Watch with second hand

PROCEDURE

1. Upon admission, set up thermometer and holder at patient's unit:
   a. Fill thermometer holder (protective container from a 2 1/2 cc. disposable syringe) with disinfectant.
   b. Place thermometer inside container.
   c. Tape container to head of bed or side of bedside locker.
2. When taking temperatures:
   a. Take containers for cotton balls to bedside.
   b. Tell patient what you are going to do.
   c. Remove thermometer from holder.
   d. Wipe thermometer with clean cotton ball. Discard cotton ball in waste container.
   e. Shake down thermometer mercury to 95° F.
   f. Place thermometer under patient's tongue.
   g. Follow above steps to second and third patient,
   h. Take third patient's pulse and respiration. Record results in T.P.R. book.
   i. Take pulse and respiration of second patient, record, then first patient,
   j. Remove thermometer from first patient's mouth after 3 minutes.
   k. Wipe thermometer with clean cotton ball. Discard cotton ball in waste container.
   l. Read thermometer and replace in holder. Record results in T.P.R. book,
   m. Repeat steps j through l for second and third patient.

CARE OF EQUIPMENT

1. After each use:
   a. Discard soiled cotton balls and container.
2. Weekly and when patient is discharged:
   a. Collect thermometers and holders.
   b. Disinfect thermometers as outlined on page 26.
   c. Place in new holders containing disinfectant.
   d. Discard old holders.
   e. Replace thermometers and holders at bedside.

———

C. TAKING TEMPERATURES WITH THE ELECTRONIC THERMOMETER

PURPOSE

To determine the patient's body temperature with an electronic thermometer which is a beat sending device with an accuracy of a plus or minus of .2 degrees. It utilizes a disposable probe cover and records oral and rectal temperatures within 15 seconds.

EQUIPMENT

1. Base for electronic thermometer
2. Thermometer with oral probe (sensing device)
3. Rectal probes where applicable
4. Disposable probe covers

PROCEDURE

1. Remove probe from base which is connected to electricity.
2. Attach strap of thermometer around shoulder to secure thermometer to side (left side if right handed).
3. Remove probe and insert probe into disposable probe cover.
4. Turn thermometer on by pressing small bar on top.
5. Place covered probe into patient's mouth in the sublingual area and slowly push probe along the base of the tongue as far back as possible without discomfort to the patient.
6. Hold probe in place until indicator on thermometer records a completed thermometer reading.
7. Transfer reading to appropriate records.
8. Eject the disposable probe cover.
9. Press bar on back of thermometer erasing present reading and repeat the above procedure for the next patient.
10. Remove thermometer pack and replace securely in base for recharging thermometer.

POINTS TO EMPHASIZE

1. Grasp probe at reinforced area in the center to decrease breakage.
2. Always keep base plugged into electrical current.
3. Always keep thermometer in base when not in use to keep the battery charged.
4. Use specified probe for rectal temperature and insert probe cover 1/2 inch on adults or 1/4 inch on babies for accurate recordings.
5. For axillary temperatures do not press bar to activate thermometer until the oral probe with cover is in place, then allow 60-90 seconds for recording of temperature. Indicator will not come on.

II. <u>TAKING AXILLARY TEMPERATURE</u>

PURPOSE

To determine a patient's temperature when the oral or rectal route is contraindicated.

EQUIPMENT

Oral thermometer tray
T.P.R. book
Pencil or pen
Watch with a second hand

PROCEDURE

Same as for oral temperature (pages 1 and 2) except:

1. Wipe axilla dry.
2. Place oral thermometer in axilla. Have patient cross arms over chest.
3. Leave thermometer in place for 10 minutes.
4. Write "A" above temperature in T.P.R. book, and T.P.R. graph (SF 511).

III. TAKING RECTAL TEMPERATURE
A. THERMOMETERS DISINFECTED ON WARD

PURPOSE

To determine patient's temperature when the oral method is contraindicated.

EQUIPMENT

1. Tray containing
   a. Two containers of disinfecting agent marked #1 and #2
   b. Container of green soap solution
   c. Container of water
   d. Container of clean cotton sponges
   e. Container for waste cotton sponges
   f. Minimum of 4 thermometers in container #1 of disinfecting agent. (Number of thermometers determined by ward needs).
   g. Tube of water soluble lubricant
   h. T.P.R. book
   i. Pencil and pen
   j. Watch with second hand

PROCEDURE

1. Take equipment to bedside.
2. Tell patient what you are going to do.
3. Remove thermometer from container fl.
4. Wipe thermometer (over waste container) with water moistened sponge from stem to bulb using a rotary motion. Discard sponge in waste container.
5. Shake thermometer mercury to 95° F.
6. Lubricate thermometer with water soluble lubricant.
7. Turn patient on side unless contraindicated.
8. Separate buttocks and gently insert thermometer 1 1/2 inches into the rectum in an upward and forward direction. Insert 1/2 - 3/4 inch in infants and children.
9. Hold thermometer in place for 5 minutes. Count pulse and respiration and record in T.P.R. book.
10. Remove thermometer.
11. Wash thermometer (over waste container) with soap moistened sponge from stem to bulb using rotary motion. Discard sponge in waste container.
12. Moisten cotton sponge with water and wipe thermometer from stem to bulb in a rotary motion. Discard sponge in waste container.
13. Read thermometer and record temperature in T.P.R. book. Place "R" above recording to indicate that it was taken rectally.
14. Return thermometer to glass #2 for sterilization for a minimum of 20 minutes.
15. Leave patient in comfortable position.

16.   Record T.P.R.'s on SF 511. Use "R" to indicate rectal temperature.

17.   Continue taking additional rectal temperatures in the same manner.

CARE OF EQUIPMENT

1.   After each use
   a.   Remove waste.
   b.   Clean tray.
   c.   Transfer thermometers from container 12 to container #1 after 20 minutes has elapsed.
   d.   Replace water and soap solution.
   e.   Reset tray.
2.   Daily
   a.   Wash containers in warm, soapy water, rinse and dry.
   b.   Change all solutions.
   c.   Wash thermometers in cold, soapy water, rinse well and place in disinfectant agent.
   d.   Refill and reset tray.

POINTS TO EMPHASIZE

1.   Wait 30 minutes before taking temperature on patient who has had an enema.
2.   Use only a stub bulb thermometer expressly made for rectal use.
3.   Do not leave patient unattended while thermometer is inserted.
4.   Report abnormal vital signs to Charge Nurse.
5.   Describe the quality of pulse and respirations in observation column on Nursing Notes (SF 510). On wards where many rectal temperatures are taken, (for example, Pediatrics, ICU, etc.), increase the number of thermometers in each container. Continue using thermometers from alternate containers, allowing at least 20 minutes for sterilization, until all patients' temperatures are taken.
6.   Be sure to rinse thermometer well before putting it into the disinfectant, as bacterial action is nullified in the presence of soap - for example, Zephiran chloride and iodine preparations.

B. THERMOMETERS DISINFECTED IN CENTRAL SUPPLY ROOM

EQUIPMENT

1.   Tray containing
   a.   Container of rectal thermometers sealed in paper envelopes
   b.   Container of clean cotton sponges
   c.   Container of soap solution
   d.   Container for waste cotton sponges
   e.   Container for used thermometers
   f.   Tube of water soluble lubricant

g. T.P.R. book
h. Pencil or pen
i. Watch with second hand

PROCEDURE
1. Remove thermometer from envelope.
2. Take, record and report vital signs as in previous procedure page 30.
3. Return thermometer to container of soap solution for return to C.S.R.

CARE OF EQUIPMENT
1. After each use
   Remove waste
   Clean tray
2. Daily
   Return container of thermometers to C.S.R.in accordance with local instructions and exchange for supply of sterile thermometers.
   Wash containers in warm/ soapy water, rinse and dry.
   Refill and reset tray.

IV. TAKING PULSE AND RESPIRATION

PURPOSE

To determine the character and rate of the pulse and respiration.

EQUIPMENT
Watch with a second hand
Pencil or pen
T. P. R. book

PROCEDURE
1. Tell patient what he is to do.
2. Have the patient lie down or sit in chair. Draw his arm and hand across his chest.
3. Place three fingers over the radial artery on the thumb side of the patient's wrist. Use just enough pressure to feel the pulse beat.
4. Observe the general character of the pulse, then count the number of beats for 30 seconds, multiply by two. If any deviation from normal or irregularity is noted, count for one full minute.
5. With the fingers still on the wrist, count the rise and fall of the chest or upper abdomen for 30 seconds, multiply by 2. If any irregularity or difficulty is noted, count for one full minute.
5. Record in T. P. R. book and report any abnormality.

POINTS TO EMPHASIZE
DO NOT use thumb when taking pulse beat.

V. <u>APICAL-RADIAL PULSE</u>

PURPOSE

To compare the pulse rate of the heart at the apex and the pulse rate in the radial artery.

EQUIPMENT

Stethoscope

Watch with second hand

PROCEDURE

1. Tell patient what you are going to do.
2. Have patient lie quietly in bed.
3. Open pajama coat to expose chest.
4. One person standing on the left side of the bed places a stethoscope over apex of heart (slightly below and to the right of the left nipple) to locate the apical heart beat.
5. Another person standing on the right side of bed locates the radial pulse; hold watch so that it can be seen by both people.
6. Using the same watch and at a signal from the person taking the apical pulse, both people count for one minute.
7. Replace pajama coat; leave patient comfortable.
8. Record in observation column on Nursing Notes (SF 510). Example: Apical 92. Radial 86.

POINTS TO EMPHASIZE

<u>Two</u> corpsmen are necessary to carry out this procedure because the two pulses must be taken at the same time to compare rates.

CARE OF EQUIPMENT

1. Wipe earpieces and diaphragm/bell of stethoscope with alcohol sponges before and after procedure.
2. Return stethoscope to proper place.

VI. <u>TAKING BLOOD PRESSURE</u>

<u>PURPOSE</u>

To determine the pressure which the blood exerts against the walls of the vessels.

<u>EQUIPMENT</u>

Sphygmomanometer
Stethoscope
Pencil and paper
Alcohol sponges

<u>PROCEDURE</u>

1. Tell patient what you are going to do.
2. Place patient in comfortable position sitting or lying down.
3. Place rubber portion of cuff over the brachial artery. Secure either by hooking or wrapping depending on the type of apparatus.
4. Clip indicator to cuff (aneroid) or place apparatus on a level surface (mercury) at about heart level. Make sure the tubing is not kinked and that it does not rub against the apparatus.
5. Locate brachial pulse at bend of elbow.
6. Place stethoscope in ears with ear pieces pointing forward.
7. Hold stethoscope in place over the brachial artery. Inflate cuff until the indicator registers 200 mm. Loosen thumb screw of valve and allow air to escape slowly.
8. Listen for the sounds. Watch the indicator. Note where the first distinct rhythmic sound is heard. This is the Systolic Pressure.
9. Continue releasing air from the cuff. Note where sound changes to dull muffled beat. This is the <u>Diastolic Pressure.</u>
10. Open valve completely. Release all air from cuff.
11. Remove cuff. Record reading.

<u>POINTS TO EMPHASIZE</u>

1. Either arm may be used in taking blood pressure, but in repeating readings, it is important to use the same arm.
2. Some departments in the hospital may define diastolic pressure as the last sound heard.
3. If unsure of reading, completely deflate cuff and repeat procedure.

<u>CARE OF EQUIPMENT</u>

1. Fold and replace cuff.
2. Wipe ear pieces and bell/diaphragm of stethoscope with alcohol sponge before and after procedure. Replace.

VII . RECORDING ON THE TEMPERATURE, PULSE, AND RESPIRATION FORM

PURPOSE

To keep an accurate and up-to-date record of the patient's cardinal or vital signs.

EQUIPMENT

Pen with black or blue-black ink
Standard Form 511, Temperature–Pulse–Respiration
Ruler
Addressograph plate

PROCEDURE

1. Complete identifying data in lower left corner of SF-511.
2. Fill in spaces as indicated in the heading by printing:
    Month
    Date of month.
    Hospital day.
    Postoperative or postpartum day.
    Hours T.P.R's are taken.
3. Using a small dot, record temperature and pulse in spaces corresponding vertically to hour and horizontally to scales on left side of form. Join dots of previous readings by drawing straight lines with ruler.
4. Print respiration rate in space indicated to correspond with date and hour taken.
5. Record blood pressure in space indicated to correspond with date and hour taken.
6. Record height and weight on admission in spaces provided. Repeated weight recordings are made to correspond with date and hour taken.

POINTS TO EMPHASIZE

1. For every four hour and twice a day temperature and pulse, record within dotted lines.
2. For four times a day temperature and pulse, record on dotted lines.
3. Blood pressures required more than twice a day should be graphed on a Plotting Chart (SF 512).
4. Any pecularities of the patient that affects the temperature, pulse, or respiration, i.e.; drop in temperature due to medication; ongoing cooling procedure; and/or absences from ward, may be recorded in ..graphic column at the designated time.
5. Indicate method - if axillary or rectal is used.

———————

14

SAMPLE TEMPERATURE - PULSE -RESPIRATION (SF511)

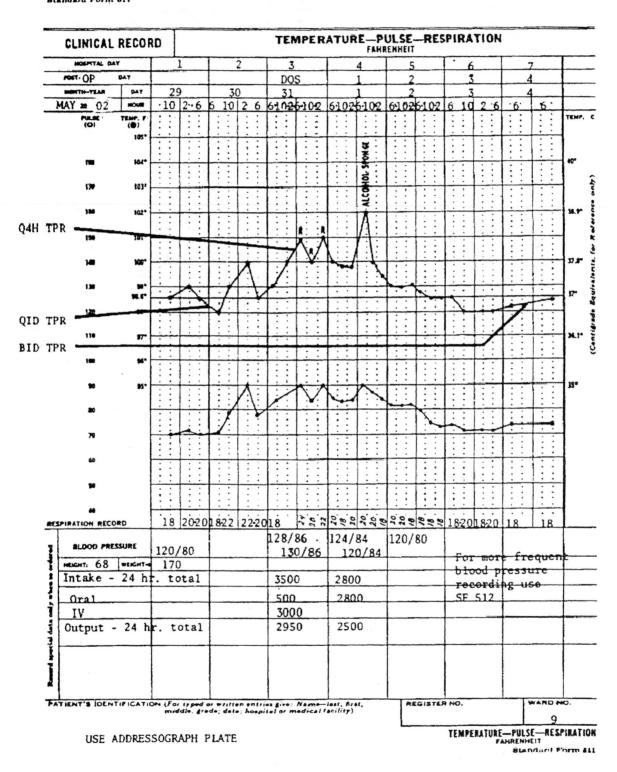

USE ADDRESSOGRAPH PLATE

15

USING THE TEMPERATURE - PULSE - RESPIRATION
GRAPHIC FORM 511

All entries shall be lettered in black or blue-black ink. Ballpoint pens may be used. Each sheet should have identifying data at the foot of each page. These data should be legible, correct and complete.

PATIENT'S IDENTIFICATION (For typed or written entries give: Name—last, first, middle grade date, hospital or medical facility)	REGISTER NO.	WARD NO.
	006-498	9

USE ADDRESSOGRAPH PLATE

TEMPERATURE—PULSE—RESPIRATION
FAHRENHEIT
Standard Form 511

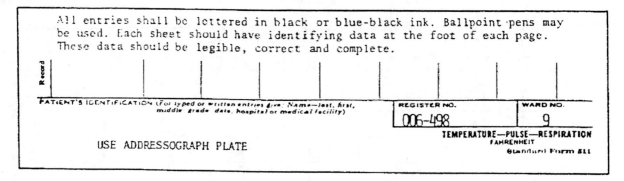

Each sheet is divided into seven major columns, one for each day of the week. The day of admission is the first hospital day.

The month, day of the month, and year appear in the spaces for that purpose. In the sample below, the patient was admitted to the hospital on May 7, 2002.

The day of operation or delivery is lettered "Operation" or "Delivery". The following day is the first postoperative or postdelivery day. For example, if the patient had surgery on his third hospital day, the chart would appear as follows:

CLINICAL RECORD

HOSPITAL DAY		1	
POST· OP DAY			
MONTH-YEAR	**DAY**	7	
MAY 2002	**HOUR**	·6·	·6·

PULSE (O)	TEMP. F (●)		
	105°		
160	104°		
170	103°		
160	102°		
150	101°		
140	100°		
130	99°		
	98.6°		
120	98°		
110	97°		
100	96°		
90	95°		
80			
70			
60			
50			
40			
RESPIRATION RECORD		16	18

To chart the temperature and pulse, place a dot on the graph according to the scale on the left in the vertical column that designates the correct time and date. Connect the dot of the previous recording with a solid line.

The respirations are recorded in the vertical column according to the hour.

In the sample at the left the 6 a.m. TPR was 97-72-16. The 6 p.m. TPR was 98.6-76-18.

Each day is divided into two columns, a.m. and p.m.

CLINICAL RECORD		TEMPERATURE—PULSE—RESPIRATION FAHRENHEIT							
HOSPITAL DAY		1	2	3	4	5	6	7	
POST- OP DAY				DOS	1	2	3	4	
MONTH-YEAR DAY		7	8	9	10	11	12	13	
MAY 28 02 HOUR									
PULSE (O)	TEMP. F									TEMP. C

a.m. p.m.

The a.m. and p.m. subdivision is further divided by two vertical dotted lines. For every four hour temperature and pulse reading, place the recordings WITHIN the dotted lines.

CLINICAL RECORD		TEMPERATURE—PULSE—RESPIRATION FAHRENHEIT							
HOSPITAL DAY		1	2	3	4	5	6	7	
POST- OP DAY				DOS	1	2	3	4	
MONTH-YEAR DAY		7	8	9	10	11	12	13	
MAY 28 02 HOUR		2·6·10	2·6·10	2·6·10	2·6·10	2·6·10	2·6·10	2·6·10	
PULSE (♡)	TEMP. F (●)									TEMP. C

2 a.m.   10 p.m.
6 a.m.   6 p.m.
10 a.m.   2 p.m.

Twice a day temperature and pulse recordings are placed WITHIN the dotted lines in the center of the a.m. and p.m. column.

CLINICAL RECORD		TEMPERATURE—PULSE—RESPIRATION FAHRENHEIT							
HOSPITAL DAY		1	2	3	4	5	6	7	
POST- OP DAY				DOS	1	2	3	4	
MONTH-YEAR DAY		7	8	9	10	11	12	13	
MAY 28 02 HOUR		·6· ·6·	·6· ·6·	·6· ·6·	·6· ·6·	·6· ·6·	·6· ·6·	·6· ·6·	
PULSE (O)	TEMP. F (●)									TEMP.

6 a.m.   6 p.m.

For four-times-a-day readings, place the recordings ON the dotted lines.

CLINICAL RECORD		TEMPERATURE—PULSE—RESPIRATION FAHRENHEIT							
HOSPITAL DAY		1	2	3	4	5	6	7	
POST- OP DAY				DOS	1	2	3	4	
MONTH-YEAR DAY		7	8	9	10	11	12	13	
MAY 28 02 HOUR		6 10 2 6	6 10 2 6	6 10 2 6	6 10 2 6	6 10 2 6	6 10 2 6	6 10 2 6	
PULSE	TEMP. F									TEMP. C

6 a.m.   6 p.m.
10 a.m.   2 p.m.

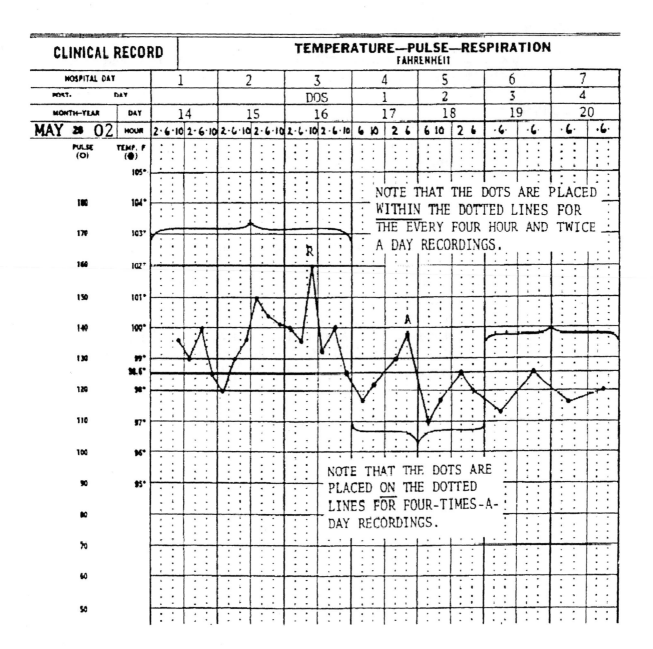

If a temperature is taken by rectum, place an "R" (for rectal) above the dot on the graph.
If a temperature is taken by axilla, place an "A" (for axillary) above the dot on the graph.

VIII. <u>RECORDING ON PLOTTING CHART</u>

<u>PURPOSE</u>

To keep an accurate, visible record of repeated observations of intake-output, weight, blood pressure, etc.

<u>EQUIPMENT</u>

Pen with, black or blue-black ink
Standard Form 512, Plotting Chart
Ruler

<u>PROCEDURE</u>

1. Complete identifying data in lower left corner of chart. (Page 25)
2. Print date and purpose in upper left corner.
3. Calibrate measurements along vertical portion of graph:
   Start scale at bottom working toward top at a definite and uniform rate of progression, as 0-10-20.30.
   Label scale at top to show unit of measure as cc. , lbs. , or mm.
4. Note date time intervals of measure along top horizontal portion of graph.
5. Show meaning of symbols used in a key to the side of graph.

<u>Note:</u> Red pencil may be ued when filling in bar graphs.

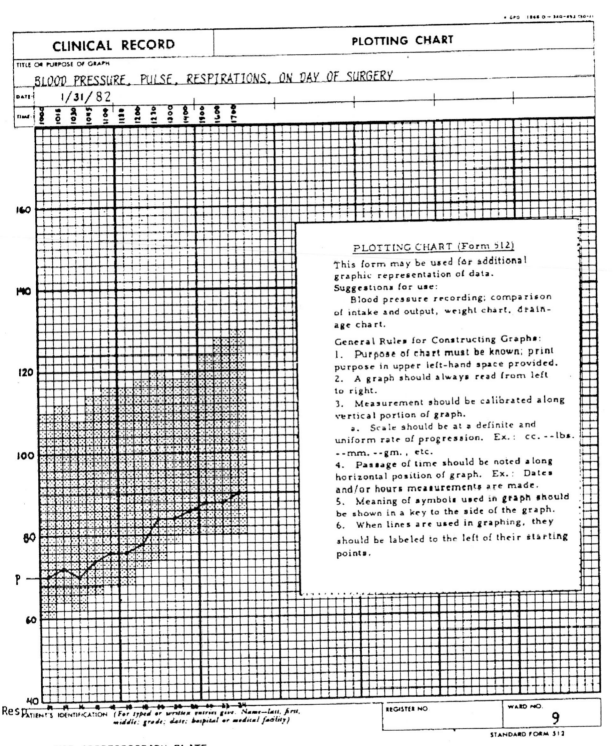

* GPO 1846 0 - 340-493 (50-1)

CLINICAL RECORD	PLOTTING CHART

TITLE OR PURPOSE OF GRAPH

BLOOD PRESSURE, PULSE, RESPIRATIONS, ON DAY OF SURGERY

DATE: 1/31/82

PLOTTING CHART (Form 512)

This form may be used for additional graphic representation of data.
Suggestions for use:

Blood pressure recording; comparison of intake and output, weight chart, drainage chart.

General Rules for Constructing Graphs:
1. Purpose of chart must be known; print purpose in upper left-hand space provided.
2. A graph should always read from left to right.
3. Measurement should be calibrated along vertical portion of graph.
   a. Scale should be at a definite and uniform rate of progression. Ex.: cc.--lbs. --mm.--gm., etc.
4. Passage of time should be noted along horizontal position of graph. Ex.: Dates and/or hours measurements are made.
5. Meaning of symbols used in graph should be shown in a key to the side of the graph.
6. When lines are used in graphing, they should be labeled to the left of their starting points.

PATIENT'S IDENTIFICATION (For typed or written entries give: Name—last, first, middle; grade; date; hospital or medical facility)

REGISTER NO	WARD NO.
	9

STANDARD FORM 512

USE ADDRESSOGRAPH PLATE

COMMON DIAGNOSTIC NORMS

CONTENTS

Page

COMMON DIAGNOSTIC NORMS

1. RESPIRATION: From 16-20 per minute.

2. PULSE-RATE: Men, about 72 per minute.
                    Women, about 80 per minute.

3. BLOOD PRESSURE:
    Men: 110-135 (Systolic)   Women: 95-125   (Systolic)
           70-85   (Diastolic)   65-70   (Diastolic)

4. BASAL METABOLISM: Represents the body energy expended to maintain respiration, circulation, etc. Normal rate ranges from plus 10 to minus 10.

5. BLOOD:

    a. Red Blood (Erythrocyte) Count:
    Male adult - 5,000,000 per cu. mm.
    Female adult - 4,500,000 per cu. mm.
        (Increased in polycythemia vera, poisoning by carbon monoxide, in chronic pulmonary artery sclerosis, and in concentration of blood by sweating, vomiting, or diarrhea.)
        (Decreased in pernicious anemia, secondary anemia, and hypochronic anemia.)
    b. White Blood (Leukocyte) Count: 6,000 to 8,000 per cu. mm.
        (Increased with muscular exercise, acute infections, intestinal obstruction, coronary thrombosis, leukemias.)
        (Decreased due to injury to source of blood formation and interference in delivery of cells to bloodstream, typhoid, pernicious anemia, arsenic and benzol poisoning.)
        The total leukocyte group is made up of a number of diverse varieties of white blood cells. Not only the total leukocyte count, but also the relative count of the diverse varieties, is an important aid to diagnosis. In normal blood, from:
        70-72% of the leukocytes are *polymorphonuclear neuirophils.*
        2-4% of the leukocytes are *polymorphonuclear eosinophils.*
        0-.5% of the leukocytes are *basophils,*
        20-25% of the leukocytes are *lymphocytes.*
        2-6% of the leukocytes are *monocytes.*
    c. Blood Platelet (Thrombocyte) Count:
        250,000 per cu. mm. Blood platelets are important in blood coagulation.

    d. Hemoglobin Content:
        May normally vary from 85-100%. A 100% hemoglobin content is equivalent to the presence of 15.6 grams of hemoglobin in 100 c.c. of blood.
    e. Color Index:
        Represents the relative amount of hemoglobin contained in a red blood corpuscle compared with that of a normal individual of the patient's age and sex.
        The normal is 1. To determine the color index, the percentage of hemoglobin is divided by the ratio of red cells in the patient's blood to a norm of 5,000,000.
        Thus, a hemoglobin content of 60% and a red cell count of 4,000,000 (80% of 5,000,000) produces an abnormal color index of .75.

f. Sedimentation Rate:
  Represents the measurement of the speed with which red cells settle toward the bottom of a containing vessel. The rate is expressed in millimeters per hour, and indicates the total sedimentation of red blood cells at the end of 60 minutes.

Average rate:	4-7 mm. in 1 hour
Slightly abnormal rate:	8-15 mm. in 1 hour
Moderately abnormal rate:	16-40 mm. in 1 hour
Considerably abnormal rate:	41-80 mm. in 1 hour

  (The sedimentation rate is above normal in patients with chronic infections, or in whom there is a disease process involving destruction of tissue, such as coronary thrombosis, etc.)

g. Blood Sugar:
  90-120 mg. per 100 c.c. (Normal)
  In mild diabetics: 150-300 mg. per 100 c.c.
  In severe diabetics: 300-1200 mg. per 100 c.c.

h. Blood Lead:
  0.1 mg. or less in 100 c.c. (Normal). Greatly increased in lead poisoning.

i. Non-Protein Nitrogen:
  Since the function of the kidneys is to remove from the blood certain of the waste products of cellular activity, any degree of accumulation of these waste products in the blood is a measure of renal malfunction. For testing purposes, the substances chosen for measurement are the nitrogen-containing products of protein combustion, their amounts being estimated in terms of the nitrogen they contain. These substances are urea, uric acid, and creatinine, the sum total of which, in addition to any traces of other waste products, being designated as total non-protein nitrogen (NPN).

  The normal limits of NPN in 100 c.c. of blood range from 25-40 mg. Of this total, urea nitrogen normally constitutes 12-15 mg., uric acid 2-4 mg., and creatinine 1-2 mg.

6. URINE:

  a. Urine - Lead:
    0.08 mg. per liter of urine (normal).
    (Increased in lead poisoning.)

  b. Sugar:
    From none to a faint trace (normal).
    From 0.5% upwards (abnormal).
    (Increased in diabetes mellitus.)

  c. Urea:
    Normal excretion ranges from 15-40 grams in 24 hours.
    (Increased in fever and toxic states.)

  d. Uric Acid:
    Normal excretion is variable. (Increased in leukemia and gout.)

  e. Albumin:
    Normal renal cells allow a trace of albumin to pass into the urine, but this trace is so minute that it cannot be detected by ordinary tests.

f. Casts:
In some abnormal conditions, the kidney tubules become lined with substances which harden and form a mould or *oast* inside the tubes. These are later washed out by the urine, and may be detected microscopically. They are named either from the substance composing them, or from their appearance. Thus, there are pus casts, epithelial casts from the walls of the tubes, hyaline casts formed from coagulable elements of the blood, etc.

g. Pus Cells:
These are found in the urine in cases of nephritis or other inflammatory conditions of the urinary tract.

h. Epithelial Cells:
These are always present in the urine. Their number is greatly multiplied, however, in inflammatory conditions of the urinary tract.

i. Specific Gravity:
This is the ratio between the weight of a given volume of urine to that of the same volume of water. A normal reading ranges from 1.015 to 1.025. A high specific gravity usually occurs in diabetes mellitus. A low specific gravity is associated with a polyuria.

7. SPINAL FLUID:

a. Spinal Fluid Pressure (Manometric Reading):
100-200 mm. of water or 7-15 mm, of mercury (normal).
(Increased in cerebral edema, cerebral hemorrhage, meningitis, certain brain tumors, or if there is some process blocking the fluid circulation in the spinal column, such as a tumor or herniated nucleus pulposus impinging on the spinal canal.)

b. Quickenstedt's Sign:
When the veins in the neck are compressed on one or both sides, there is a rapid rise in the pressure of the cerebrospinal fluid of healthy persons, and this rise quickly disappears when pressure is removed from the neck. But when there is a block of the vertebral canal, the pressure of the cerebrospinal fluid is little or not at all affected by this maneuver.

c. Cerebrospinal Sugar:
50-60 mg. per 100 c.c. of spinal fluid (normal).
(Increased in epidemic encephalitis, diabetes mellitus, and increased intracranial pressure.)
(Decreased in purulent and tuberculous meningitis.)

d. Cerebrospinal Protein:
15-40 mg. per 100 c.c. of spinal fluid (normal).
(Increased in suppurative meningitis, epileptic seizures, cerebrospinal syphilis, anterior poliomyelitis, brain abscess, and brain tumor.)

e. Colloidal Gold Test:
This test is made to determine the presence of cerebrospinal protein.

f. Cerebrospinal Cell Count:
0-10 lymphocytes per cu. mm. (normal).

g. Cerebrospinal Globulin:
Normally negative. It is positive in various types of meningitis, various types of syphilis of the central nervous system, in poliomyelitis, in brain tumor, and in intracranial hemorrhage.

8. SNELLEN CHART FRACTIONS AS SCHEDULE LOSS DETERMINANTS:

    a. Visual acuity is expressed by a Snell Fraction, where the numerator represents the distance, in feet, between the subject and the test chart, and the denominator represents the distance, in feet, at which a normal eye could read a type size which the abnormal eye can read only at 20 feet.

    b. Thus, 20/20 means that an individual placed 20 feet from the test chart clearly sees the size of type that one with normal vision should see at that distance.

    c. 20/60 means that an individual placed 20 feet from the test chart can read only a type size, at a distance of 20 feet, which one of normal vision could read at 60 feet.

    d. Reduction of a Snellen Fraction to its simplest form roughly indicates the amount of vision remaining in an eye. Thus, a visual acuity of 20/60 corrected implies a useful vision of 1/3 or 33 1/3%, and a visual loss of 2/3 or 66 2/3% of the eye.

Similarly:

Visual Acuity (Corrected)	Percentage Loss of Use of Eye
20/20	No loss
20/25	20%
20/30	33 1/3%
20/40	50%
20/50	60%
20/60	66 2/3%
20/70	70% (app.)
20/80	75%
20/100	100% (since loss of 80% or more constitutes industrial blindness)

———

ANSWER SHEET

ST NO. _____ PART _____ TITLE OF POSITION _____
(AS GIVEN IN EXAMINATION ANNOUNCEMENT - INCLUDE OPTION, IF ANY)

ACE OF EXAMINATION _____ DATE _____
(CITY OR TOWN)   (STATE)

RATING

USE THE SPECIAL PENCIL.   MAKE GLOSSY BLACK MARKS.

	A B C D E		A B C D E		A B C D E		A B C D E		A B C D E
1	⁝⁝⁝⁝⁝	26	⁝⁝⁝⁝⁝	51	⁝⁝⁝⁝⁝	76	⁝⁝⁝⁝⁝	101	⁝⁝⁝⁝⁝
2	⁝⁝⁝⁝⁝	27	⁝⁝⁝⁝⁝	52	⁝⁝⁝⁝⁝	77	⁝⁝⁝⁝⁝	102	⁝⁝⁝⁝⁝
3	⁝⁝⁝⁝⁝	28	⁝⁝⁝⁝⁝	53	⁝⁝⁝⁝⁝	78	⁝⁝⁝⁝⁝	103	⁝⁝⁝⁝⁝
4	⁝⁝⁝⁝⁝	29	⁝⁝⁝⁝⁝	54	⁝⁝⁝⁝⁝	79	⁝⁝⁝⁝⁝	104	⁝⁝⁝⁝⁝
5	⁝⁝⁝⁝⁝	30	⁝⁝⁝⁝⁝	55	⁝⁝⁝⁝⁝	80	⁝⁝⁝⁝⁝	105	⁝⁝⁝⁝⁝
6	⁝⁝⁝⁝⁝	31	⁝⁝⁝⁝⁝	56	⁝⁝⁝⁝⁝	81	⁝⁝⁝⁝⁝	106	⁝⁝⁝⁝⁝
7	⁝⁝⁝⁝⁝	32	⁝⁝⁝⁝⁝	57	⁝⁝⁝⁝⁝	82	⁝⁝⁝⁝⁝	107	⁝⁝⁝⁝⁝
8	⁝⁝⁝⁝⁝	33	⁝⁝⁝⁝⁝	58	⁝⁝⁝⁝⁝	83	⁝⁝⁝⁝⁝	108	⁝⁝⁝⁝⁝
9	⁝⁝⁝⁝⁝	34	⁝⁝⁝⁝⁝	59	⁝⁝⁝⁝⁝	84	⁝⁝⁝⁝⁝	109	⁝⁝⁝⁝⁝
10	⁝⁝⁝⁝⁝	35	⁝⁝⁝⁝⁝	60	⁝⁝⁝⁝⁝	85	⁝⁝⁝⁝⁝	110	⁝⁝⁝⁝⁝

Make only ONE mark for each answer.   Additional and stray marks may be
counted as mistakes.   In making corrections, erase errors COMPLETELY.

	A B C D E		A B C D E		A B C D E		A B C D E		A B C D E
11	⁝⁝⁝⁝⁝	36	⁝⁝⁝⁝⁝	61	⁝⁝⁝⁝⁝	86	⁝⁝⁝⁝⁝	111	⁝⁝⁝⁝⁝
12	⁝⁝⁝⁝⁝	37	⁝⁝⁝⁝⁝	62	⁝⁝⁝⁝⁝	87	⁝⁝⁝⁝⁝	112	⁝⁝⁝⁝⁝
13	⁝⁝⁝⁝⁝	38	⁝⁝⁝⁝⁝	63	⁝⁝⁝⁝⁝	88	⁝⁝⁝⁝⁝	113	⁝⁝⁝⁝⁝
14	⁝⁝⁝⁝⁝	39	⁝⁝⁝⁝⁝	64	⁝⁝⁝⁝⁝	89	⁝⁝⁝⁝⁝	114	⁝⁝⁝⁝⁝
15	⁝⁝⁝⁝⁝	40	⁝⁝⁝⁝⁝	65	⁝⁝⁝⁝⁝	90	⁝⁝⁝⁝⁝	115	⁝⁝⁝⁝⁝
16	⁝⁝⁝⁝⁝	41	⁝⁝⁝⁝⁝	66	⁝⁝⁝⁝⁝	91	⁝⁝⁝⁝⁝	116	⁝⁝⁝⁝⁝
17	⁝⁝⁝⁝⁝	42	⁝⁝⁝⁝⁝	67	⁝⁝⁝⁝⁝	92	⁝⁝⁝⁝⁝	117	⁝⁝⁝⁝⁝
18	⁝⁝⁝⁝⁝	43	⁝⁝⁝⁝⁝	68	⁝⁝⁝⁝⁝	93	⁝⁝⁝⁝⁝	118	⁝⁝⁝⁝⁝
19	⁝⁝⁝⁝⁝	44	⁝⁝⁝⁝⁝	69	⁝⁝⁝⁝⁝	94	⁝⁝⁝⁝⁝	119	⁝⁝⁝⁝⁝
20	⁝⁝⁝⁝⁝	45	⁝⁝⁝⁝⁝	70	⁝⁝⁝⁝⁝	95	⁝⁝⁝⁝⁝	120	⁝⁝⁝⁝⁝
21	⁝⁝⁝⁝⁝	46	⁝⁝⁝⁝⁝	71	⁝⁝⁝⁝⁝	96	⁝⁝⁝⁝⁝	121	⁝⁝⁝⁝⁝
22	⁝⁝⁝⁝⁝	47	⁝⁝⁝⁝⁝	72	⁝⁝⁝⁝⁝	97	⁝⁝⁝⁝⁝	122	⁝⁝⁝⁝⁝
23	⁝⁝⁝⁝⁝	48	⁝⁝⁝⁝⁝	73	⁝⁝⁝⁝⁝	98	⁝⁝⁝⁝⁝	123	⁝⁝⁝⁝⁝
24	⁝⁝⁝⁝⁝	49	⁝⁝⁝⁝⁝	74	⁝⁝⁝⁝⁝	99	⁝⁝⁝⁝⁝	124	⁝⁝⁝⁝⁝
25	⁝⁝⁝⁝⁝	50	⁝⁝⁝⁝⁝	75	⁝⁝⁝⁝⁝	100	⁝⁝⁝⁝⁝	125	⁝⁝⁝⁝⁝

ANSWER SHEET

PART _____ TITLE OF POSITION _____

(AS GIVEN IN EXAMINATION ANNOUNCEMENT - INCLUDE OPTION, IF ANY)

PLACE OF EXAMINATION _____ DATE _____

(CITY OR TOWN)   (STATE)

RATING

USE THE SPECIAL PENCIL. MAKE GLOSSY BLACK MARKS.

	A B C D E		A B C D E		A B C D E		A B C D E		A B C D E
1		26		51		76		101	
2		27		52		77		102	
3		28		53		78		103	
4		29		54		79		104	
5		30		55		80		105	
6		31		56		81		106	
7		32		57		82		107	
8		33		58		83		108	
9		34		59		84		109	
10		35		60		85		110	

Make only ONE mark for each answer.   Additional and stray marks may be counted as mistakes.   In making corrections, erase errors COMPLETELY.

	A B C D E		A B C D E		A B C D E		A B C D E		A B C D E
11		36		61		86		111	
12		37		62		87		112	
13		38		63		88		113	
14		39		64		89		114	
15		40		65		90		115	
16		41		66		91		116	
17		42		67		92		117	
18		43		68		93		118	
19		44		69		94		119	
20		45		70		95		120	
21		46		71		96		121	
22		47		72		97		122	
23		48		73		98		123	
24		49		74		99		124	
25		50		75		100		125	